RETHINKING CONSUMER
DATA AND BEHAVIOR

CONSUMER CORNER SERIES
UNCONVENTIONAL LESSONS FROM
CONSUMER BEHAVIOR

Why do consumers make the choices they do, and what can those choices teach us? The Consumer Corner series explores the subtle forces that shape consumer behavior, across topics that range from food, retail, health, vacations, and more. By spotlighting overlooked, counterintuitive, or nontraditional insights, the series challenges standard economic thinking and highlights the messy, human side of decision-making that sometimes occurs when humans engage in the marketplace. Drawing on behavioral science, lived experiences, and industry expertise, this series reveals what people can teach us as they make complex choices across the supply chain.

SERIES EDITOR

Nicole J. Olynk Widmar
Professor and Head of the Department Agricultural Economics
Purdue University

OTHER TITLES IN THIS SERIES

Decisions That Shape Supply Chains
Markets We Thought We Knew
Consumer Lessons From a Pandemic
Market Signals From Online Behavior

RETHINKING CONSUMER DATA AND BEHAVIOR

NICOLE J. OLYNK WIDMAR
MICHAEL L. SMITH
ERIN ROBINSON

Purdue University Press
West Lafayette, Indiana

978-1-62671-317-8 (paperback)
978-1-62671-318-5 (epdf)

Cover image: Hand Smashes Piggy Bank With Hammer, Scattering Coins Across Modern
Office Desk, Symbolizing Financial Urgency, Emergency Fund Usage, and the Importance
of Savings and Budgeting: gorodenkoff/iStock via Getty Images Plus

CONTENTS

INTRODUCTION

Rethinking Consumer Data and Behavior

Consumer Corner is about understanding why consumers make the choices they do—and what we can learn from those choices. We draw on behavioral sciences, lived experiences, industry experience, markets, and societal events (lessons from a pandemic, anyone?) to explore the complexities of decision-making.

In Book One, we examined how the choices we make shape the supply chains in our food and agricultural industries. Book Two revisited markets that we thought we knew, until they experienced an unforeseen (or even a foreseen) shock. Book Three begrudgingly revisited what we learned (and perhaps what we hope we can unlearn) from COVID-19. In Book Four, we turned to online and social media as portholes into what consumers and the public were thinking. These platforms provide new data sources with real-time potential, but they also come with challenges—messy, noisy, and sometimes misleading.

Now we arrive at *Rethinking Consumer Data and Behavior*. After all, rethinking and revisiting previous notions is what we do here. How can we not question the data we rely on so heavily after raising so many questions about its use, origin, and the intent behind its analysis?

This book examines data collected from individuals (surveys), from social media (the polished, public-facing version of ourselves), from news media, and from passive sources like smart devices. We check boxes allowing our data to be collected, stored, or even shared. But few of us read the fine print before clicking *next*. Every day, we create data through our movements at home, in vehicles (which have the capacity to send you an email reminder that they need servicing or notice something is awry), and in our work environments.

We're aware when we complete a survey or answer questions about an experience. But we rarely think twice about what we type into the Google search bar because the benefits—an answer—outweigh the cost. In doing so, we contribute to aggregate search trends, joining a collective online society. Posting on social media makes this even more explicit; the world can see what we share, even if some people remain shocked at the consequences.

You have probably heard the saying: "Water, water, everywhere, but not a drop to drink." The original quote from Coleridge's *The Rime of the Ancient Mariner* (1834) is a bit more nuanced:

> *Water, water, every where,*
> *And all the boards did shrink;*
> *Water, water, every where,*
> *Nor any drop to drink.*

The poem refers to mariners surrounded by water they could not drink—a situation easily extended to today's data environment. We are quite literally surrounded by data, datasets, databases—you name it. Your phone generates data about you, by you, and for you. Your smart appliances have data about usage and might even email you when they need servicing. Your iPhone, sleeping peacefully next to your head, maybe mere inches away from your head (a separate sleep-hygiene discussion for another time), never really sleeps. It anticipates your alarm, updates your apps, and waits for your next move. You're awash in a sea of data. But does it serve you? Or are you still searching for meaningful insights?

We used to complain that we didn't know enough. Now we know, or can know, almost anything. If we don't, Siri or Alexa can. If they can't, ChatGPT or Claude will try, even if what they provide is hallucinated and not reliable without human validation. Information is no longer scarce. Instead, we risk paralysis by abundance. Data, data, everywhere, but where do we start?

The challenge isn't access to data; it's knowing what to do with it, which questions to ask, and how to navigate an overwhelming volume of possible answers. Some of it's useful. Much of it isn't. And figuring out which is which? That's the work ahead.

1

DIS/MIS-INFORMATION

Difficult to Detect, but Impossible to Ignore

BY CAMILLE (CAMI) RYAN

P icture it: You are a respected, established advocate for agriculture and food production. You might even have a well-recognized brand. You come across a post on Facebook or Twitter that contains information that is:

1. Inaccurate (not evidence- or science-based)
2. Inflammatory
3. Biased
4. Not credibly sourced
5. One, any, or all of the above

What do you do?

Those of us who have been around the "debunking" block a time or two have learned how to identify sketchy information and find ways to mitigate or debunk it. We leverage a vast network of credible experts in the area such as Jayson Lusk (agricultural economist), Lynn Sosnoskie (weed scientist), or organizations like the Cornell Alliance for Science. I've even directed family members and friends to fact-checking sites such as Snopes or Hoaxslayer when I've come across claims like "lemons will cure your cancer!" or "gargling with salt water will cure COVID-19!"

But here's another scenario: What if the source of the misinformation comes from another science- or evidence-based advocate or expert just like you?

None of us are immune to misinformation, no matter who we are or how deep our expertise runs. I've slipped up many times over the years. My cognitive traps include satire (I'm very literal), misreading intent, and failing to check background or context. I don't think I'm alone in this. We can all get tripped up by misplaced ideology or simple carelessness. And let's face it—when we do, we'll get called out. Twitter never forgets, and it rarely forgives.

But let's step back. Are you dealing with misinformation or disinformation? There is a difference.

Misinformation refers to inaccurate or incomplete information. It can mislead (Fallis 2009) through:

- An honest mistake
- Negligence
- Unconscious bias

Disinformation is qualitatively different. It is defined as "a product of a carefully planned and technically sophisticated deceit process" (Fallis 2009). Disinformation comes with intended or expected outcomes—anything from attracting likes and shares to outright bans of targeted products or technologies. Disinformation is a product with a market (Ryan et al. 2020).

The main difference between misinformation and disinformation is *intent*. But the two are inextricably intertwined. Purposeful distribution of disinformation can lead to the spread of misinformation. Conversely, misinformation can inform disinformation through strategies that exploit gaps in our understanding of products, technologies, or ideas.

As humans, we are motivated by a variety of competing factors. Branding is a big one. If someone's primary objective in posting, sharing, or tweeting is building a personal brand, it is easy to fall into the trap of sharing more inflammatory information. Inflammatory content drives attention, but it can also be purposefully sensationalized, and it can be misleading.

There are costs of mis/disinformation, such as delayed or shelved innovations (think Golden Rice or virus-resistant cassava), diminished scientific integrity (science by press conference), and the rise of predatory journals (Grudniewicz et al. 2019; Cobey 2017). This is less about scientific literacy and more about encouraging information literacy, media literacy, and critical thinking. As of 2025, an estimated 5.24 billion people across the planet use social media (DISA 2025).

No matter our level of expertise, we are social creatures, incentivized by competing factors and guilty of biased thinking. We are herd animals—all of us, including those who consider themselves knowledgeable experts. If we expect consistency in how others create, interpret, and share information, we need to do our best to inoculate ourselves against misinformation. We have to continuously demonstrate critical thinking skills, take inventory of the incentives driving our behavior, and examine the type of information shaping our beliefs. In fact, experts and advocates have the greatest responsibility to stay attuned to these spaces and be accountable when they fail or slip up.

THE AGRICULTURE ADVOCATE'S CHECKLIST:

- Understand and accept that, as an expert, you can't possibly know everything.
- Avoid snap judgments in response to mis/disinformation posts. Experts and advocates need to be "slow thinkers" (à la Daniel Kahneman).
- Constantly leverage your networks to ensure accuracy: check context, timing, dates, and intent or motivation (theirs and yours). Remember, mis- and disinformation are moving targets. It's tough to keep up.
- Share less and check more.
- Think about the collective good. Does your post or response add value to the conversation?
- Engaging in productive dialogue about agriculture means putting the relationship first. It's a conversation, not a conversion.

Finally, intent is something we must always consider when engaging in productive conversations about complex topics like GMOs, health, vaccines, or pesticides. Specific issues will come and go, but agriculture and science will always be problematized through disinformation. Fundamentally, we need to fight our urges to win today's conversation or gather attention with today's post and instead focus on building transparency and trust for the long term. Understanding the landscape of mis/disinformation—how it is created and shared, and the behaviors and biases that drive it (including our own)—is critical to ensuring that societies benefit from the best that science has to offer.

WORKS CITED

Cobey, Kelly. 2017. "Illegitimate Journals Scam Even Senior Scientists." *Nature.*

DISA. 2025. "2025 Social Network Usage and Growth Statistics." *Disinformation Social Media Alliance.* July 13. https://disa.org/2025-social-network-usage-and -growth-statistics/.

Fallis, Don. 2009. "A Conceptual Analysis of Disinformation." *iConference 2009.* University of Illinois Urbana-Champaign.

Grudniewicz, Agnes, David Moher, Kelly D. Cobey, Gregory L. Bryson, Samantha Cukier, Kristiann Allen, Clare Ardern, et al. 2019. "Predatory Journals: No Definition, No Defence." *Nature.*

Ryan, Camille D., Andrew J. Schaul, Ryan Butner, and John T. Swarthout. 2020. "Monetizing Disinformation in the Attention Economy: The Case of Genetically Modified Organisms (GMOs)." *European Management Journal* 7–18.

Adapted from original posting as *ConsumerCorner.2020.Letter.18* (https://agribusiness.purdue.edu/consumer_corner/dis-mis-information/)

2

THAT'S PROBABLY NOT A ZEBRA

BY COURTNEY BIR AND NICOLE J. OLYNK WIDMAR

***This letter is not intended to provide medical advice or interpretation of epidemiological data for seasonal influenza (flu) or COVID-19. For information on these viral diseases, please see https://www.cdc.gov/flu/index.htm *or* https://www.cdc.gov/coronavirus/2019-ncov/index.html.

A s we at *Consumer Corner* get back to our fundamentals, our guiding theme can be summed up in a few familiar idioms that point us toward the roots of consumer behavior. One of them is the classic "Keep It Simple, Silly." Yes, we are aware that the KISS mantra is keep it simple, stupid, but you know by now, at *Consumer Corner* we believe words matter. Calling people "stupid" is hardly the best way to keep you reading. After all, this focus on communication is a major theme of the first book in our series, *Consumer Corner: Decisions That Shape Supply Chains*.

In that same vein, another saying comes to mind: "When you hear hoofbeats, look for horses, not zebras." The phrase is often attributed to a 1962 article in the *Arkansas Gazette*, quoting a doctor at the University of Arkansas School of Medicine: "When you hear hoofbeats in the night, look for horses—not zebras" (Quote Investigator 2017). The original source may be questioned, but the sentiment is far reaching.

Simply stated, the idiom reminds us that when someone turns up ill, it is much more likely to be a common disease—not an exceedingly rare condition found only in medical textbooks. That principle holds across many situations.

During the height of the COVID-19 pandemic, this concept was put to the test. Public health data—such as the percentage of positive tests—was closely monitored to detect emerging hot spots (Johns Hopkins University 2025). In many cases, most testing was performed on people who already had symptoms. That means the sample was far from random, making it difficult to project those results to the entire population. When 10 percent of symptomatic individuals tested positive, the other 90 percent had symptoms caused by something else. In other words, most coughs and fevers were not COVID-19.

We also learned that pandemic illness came on top of existing illnesses rather than replacing them (US CDC 2025). People continued to experience everything from seasonal allergies to bacterial infections. Some COVID-19 precautions, such as social distancing, masking, and handwashing, contributed to a reduction in flu cases (Peek 2021).

Even so, interpreting probabilities is never easy. Rising positivity rates signaled concern for health officials, but for individuals, risk perception is fraught with a number of fallacies. We struggle to internalize probabilities, often misinterpreting or linking unrelated risks—or overlooking connections where they do exist.

The difficulty extends well beyond health. In consumer research as it pertains to agri-food businesses, we might ask: Why did consumers select food item X over food item Y? Perhaps they do not like the production practices used for food item X or have safety concerns based on rumors. Or maybe the explanation is much simpler: Food item Y simply tastes good, and that's the end of it.

The same applies in business-to-business settings. If you lose a customer to a competitor, it could be the result of an elaborate scheme by the other company to target your customers with a unique product-specific discount with a personalized, targeted marketing campaign. Or it could be that your customer saw a billboard—or simply that you failed to meet a request.

The point here? In most cases, the simplest explanation is the most likely. My money is on the horses, not zebras. But roll the dice often enough, and zebras do show up. The year 2020 brough a whole herd of novel zebras into the mix. We concoct all sorts of ideas to help ourselves process probabilities, but most of those stories rarely align with statistical truth. Does the chance of encountering a zebra go up because you recently saw one? Could it be that zebra sightings are related or driven by underlying factors (including biological processes) that are changing the probabilities in related ways? Sure. Is it likely? It depends on the situation.

All we ask is this: Keep the simple explanation on the table when answering the question, "What is going on here?"

Disclaimer: COVID-19 was a zebra—a rare, dangerous one that kicked hard. If you suspect allergies, you might be right, but testing and professional medical advice are always the best outcome.

WORKS CITED

Johns Hopkins University. 2025. "Which U.S. States Meet WHO Recommended Testing Criteria?" *Coronavirus Resource Center.* https://coronavirus.jhu.edu/testing/testing-positivity.

Peek, Katie. 2021. "Flu Has Disappeared for More Than a Year." *Scientific American.* April 29. https://www.scientificamerican.com/article/flu-has-disappeared-worldwide-during-the-covid-pandemic1/.

Quote Investigator. 2017. "Quote Origin: When You Hear Hoofbeats Look for Horses Not Zebras." quoteinvestigator.com. November 26. https://quoteinvestigator.com/2017/11/26/zebras/.

US CDC. 2025. "Excess Deaths Associated with COVID-19." *National Center for Health Statistics.* https://www.cdc.gov/nchs/nvss/vsrr/covid19/excess_deaths.htm.

Adapted from original posting as *ConsumerCorner.2020.Letter.19* (https://agribusiness.purdue.edu/consumer_corner/thats-probably-not-a-zebra/)

3

CONSIDERING CONSUMER RESEARCH

BY COURTNEY BIR

Mis- and disinformation are everywhere, as we discussed in chapter 1. This has sparked renewed interest in evaluating source material and drawing our own conclusions. When evaluating consumer studies—either the original research or popular press articles—there are a few things to keep in mind before forming opinions or accepting the conclusions others have presented to you.

The first consideration is who is doing the research and who is presenting the findings. Even good research can be presented or interpreted poorly. Does the group presenting the findings or conducting the experiment have their own motives? Even well-trained researchers, working toward unbiased answers, must take precautions to mitigate biases and carefully frame their questions. It's wise to examine results through multiple lenses.

There are many methods to elicit consumer preferences, each with their own strengths and limitations. These range from in-person experiments to scraping online data. When people think of in-person experiments, they often think about live auctions. A group of people are recruited to participate, and real money is exchanged for a product. The benefit of this type of experiment is that actual money changes hands for real products, which decreases hypothetical bias. Hypothetical bias occurs when the transaction is not a real purchase. People often struggle to internalize hypothetical purchases and may overestimate what they would pay because they are not truly considering parting with their money.

There is no perfect method. Bias potential exists in nearly all research designs. The responsibility of a good researcher is to minimize bias and disclose limitations. For example:

- In-person experiments can struggle with recruiting a diverse or representative sample.
- Online recruitment introduces sampling bias by excluding those without reliable internet access.
- Hypothetical products can't be sold in real exchanges, so studies on such products necessarily involve hypothetical scenarios.

Sample composition matters. Does the sample studied mirror the population the conclusions aim to represent? Were participants drawn from a narrow income bracket, yet conclusions applied broadly? Is the sample representative in geography, education, and gender? There is a role for state-specific assessments, or convenience sampling, but transparency about potential shortcomings is critical.

Scanner data, another popular method, captures actual purchases from large, diverse samples. The strength of scanner data is that it records real transactions. The limitation is that while we know *what* was purchased, we don't know *why*. For example, I often purchase Annie's brand cheddar bunny crackers. The data would show my demographic information (assuming I reported my own information when signing up for the shopper card instead of someone else's) and that I purchased cheddar bunnies. But why do I choose Annie's brand cheddar bunnies? Because they're organic? USDA-certified? Free of artificial flavors and synthetic colors? You get the point. The researcher doesn't know. But just for the record, I purchase them because they taste like real cheddar and are adorable.

Surveys solve some of these issues by offering controlled environments where researchers can carefully construct questions or hypothetical scenarios to minimize biases and other survey-related issues. However, surveys face their own challenges, such as survey fatigue and nonresponse bias, both of which can erode the quality of the results.

And don't forget about sample size. How many people participated? You may not calculate statistical power, but if there are only five respondents, you know that's not enough to justify broad conclusions.

My take-home message for reading or interpreting consumer research is to:

1. Read carefully.
2. Think critically about what can and cannot be inferred given the scope of the project and the sample size.
3. Consider the limitations (every study has them!), whether from framing, researcher beliefs, or imperfect strategies to mitigate bias and other data quality problems.

It takes a lot of different approaches to answer even one narrow question, and consumer behavior is constantly evolving.

—————————

Adapted from original posting as *ConsumerCorner.2020.Letter.20* (https://agribusiness.purdue.edu/consumer_corner/considering -consumer-research/)

4

AGRICULTURE AND NATURAL RESOURCES IN UNEXPECTED, "MAGICAL" PLACES

In the spring of 2020, when many US households were usually planning summer vacations, traveling to see family, and taking family trips to iconic destinations such as national parks or theme parks, travel stopped entirely. You were there—you know. If we learned anything during the stay-at-home orders of that period, it's that remaining in one place comes with significant cost. In our increasingly global lives, with business and personal travel soaring and becoming routine, the sudden halt to travel was a significant departure from the norm.

Travel, tourism, and entertainment are engrained in our lives—life's milestones often center around such experiences. Honeymoon cruise vacation complete with snorkeling in the Virgin Islands? Yes, please. High school graduation coming up for your oldest child means you should probably take a Disney World vacation to reminisce about past family travels, right? Of course. Or perhaps you prefer the polar opposite of childhood reminiscing—a trip to the Las Vegas Strip while visiting the Venetian and the Eiffel Tower in the span of an hour with a margarita in hand? Count me in.

The global travel industry has faced major disruptions, but one thing remains clear: Travel has long shaped how we form opinions, experience cultures, and see the world. Whether domestic or international, trips have historically provided opportunities to explore and learn, including exposing our families to cultures, information, experiences, and viewpoints otherwise foreign or overlooked in our daily lives.

Part of the complexity of consumers is their constant movement. But how often do we stop to think about the learning through experiences that takes place constantly around us? For example, encountering marketing messaging about natural food production in an airport advertisement, or learning about animal agriculture from an upscale restaurant menu. Conservation lessons at the local zoo align with its mission to conserve species around the globe.

As consumers, we are inundated with information in various forms wherever we go. Increasingly, people spend money on immersive experiences—trips dedicated to exploring distant lands, marveling at natural wonders, and admiring human ingenuity through architecture, art, and culture. Regardless of particular tastes and interests, the interconnectedness of our global community and our ability to travel have fed a culture that values exploration and experiential learning, even with young children in tow.

Take Disney World, for example. It features an entire park devoted to the natural world—Disney's Animal Kingdom—which pairs real animals on safari with amusing attractions like Pandora—The World of Avatar, an imaginative take on an otherworldly ecosystem. Pandora, perhaps the most unnatural of natural worlds, is a story based on valuing nature presented in a man-made environment. It's captivating both as an immersive entertainment experience and as a question about consumers' willingness to pay to for a fabricated version of nature.

Past *Consumer Corner* writings have drawn inspiration from Disney World for research, such as examining consumer perceptions via online media and considering how childhood attachments to beloved animal characters may shape our perceptions. Continuing this theme, we teamed up (Dr. Nicole J. Olynk Widmar, Dr. Courtney Bir, and McKenna Clifford) to tackle the question of whether people who had visited Walt Disney World (WDW) or SeaWorld Orlando had differing views on:

1. Agricultural and food production systems, and
2. The keeping of animals, including livestock and those for education or entertainment.

In addition to the basic question of whether residents had visited one of these two destinations, we evaluated specific attractions, particularly those focused on food production. This work built on earlier research (Bir et al. 2019).

A sample of 833 US residents were asked about their perceptions of natural resources (Bir et al. 2020). Analyses focused on Epcot and Animal Kingdom, which 84 percent and 72 percent of WDW attendees in the sample had visited in the past five years. In particular, Living with the Land, located in Future World at Epcot, was a key focal point. Other attractions that intrigued us as researchers were The Circle of Life: An Environmental Fable (since closed), Habitat Habit (Animal Kingdom), The Seas with Nemo and Friends (Epcot), and Kilimanjaro Safaris (Animal Kingdom), which has explicit antipoaching and conservation messaging.

Survey data provided insights into which attractions visitors experienced most frequently, as well as why some skipped them (see Tables 4.1 and 4.2). For example, The Seas with Nemo and Friends and Kilimanjaro Safaris ranked among the most popular attractions, while Pandora was visited less often than expected—possibly due to long wait times, crowds, or its then-recent debut.

Results indicated that entertainment value and education impact do not always align. "Living with the Land had the lowest level of agreement from respondents that the attraction was entertaining. However, it received relatively high agreement compared to other attractions for its educational value and changing visitors' views on agricultural techniques and sustainability" (Bir et al. 2019).

TABLE 4.1. *Percent of Respondents Who Visited the Attractions at Epcot and Animal Kingdom*

EPCOT (n = 131)	BRUCE'S SHARK WORLD	THE CIRCLE OF LIFE: AN ENVIRONMENTAL FABLE	LIVING WITH THE LAND	THE SEAS WITH NEMO AND FRIENDS	TURTLE TALK WITH CRUSH	I DID NOT VISIT ANY OF THESE ATTRACTIONS
% respondents visiting	23%	35%	34%	50%	27%	37%

ANIMAL KINGDOM (n = 113)	CONSERVATION STATION	HABITAT HABIT	IT'S TOUGH TO BE A BUG	KILIMANJARO SAFARIS	PANDORA—THE WORLD OF AVATAR	I DID NOT VISIT ANY OF THESE ATTRACTIONS
% respondents visiting	46%	35%	46%	56%	34%	21%

Table from Bir et al. (2019). Published full-length paper available here (https://www.tandfonline.com/doi/abs/10.1080/1752403z.2019.1601634).

TABLE 4.2. *Why Respondents Did Not Visit an Attraction*
(percentage reflects the proportion of those who did not visit)

	IT WAS NOT APPEALING TO ME	THE WAIT WAS TOO LONG	I DID NOT KNOW THE ATTRACTION EXISTED	I'M NOT SURE	I RAN OUT OF TIME	IT WAS NOT BUILT WHEN I VISITED	IT WAS CLOSED DURING MY VISIT
EPCOT ATTRACTIONS (n = 131)							
Bruce's Shark World	14%	11%	31%	20%	11%	7%	7%
The Circle of Life: An Environmental Fable	11%	11%	26%	18%	22%	8%	5%
Living with the Land	17%	17%	24%	15%	17%	5%	5%
The Seas with Nemo and Friends	12%	17%	18%	15%	23%	8%	6%
Turtle Talk with Crush	21%	11%	21%	21%	16%	3%	7%
ANIMAL KINGDOM ATTRACTIONS (n = 113)							
Conservation Station	10%	12%	18%	16%	30%	7%	6%
Habitat Habit	12%	13%	18%	23%	23%	8%	4%
It's Tough to Be a Bug	22%	15%	9%	12%	31%	1%	9%
Kilimanjaro Safaris	16%	19%	14%	9%	33%	5%	4%
Pandora—The World of Avatar	11%	14%	10%	6%	24%	4%	3%

Table from Bir et al. (2019).

USDA scientists conduct experiments in aquaculture, aeroponics, and greenhouse techniques inside Living with the Land. On a gentle, narrated boat ride, visitors can learn about these new advancements while being entertained by living Mickey Mouse–shaped art and a variety of impeccably groomed and designed landscapes. People have generally enjoyed witnessing agricultural advancements and idyllic farming.

"Until 1996, WDW's Magic Kingdom was home to Grandma Duck's Petting Farm" (Korkis, 2015). The beloved farmyard animals of Grandma Duck were available for people to interact with through petting and feeding. The star of the barnyard was the famous Minnie Moo, a Holstein with a very clear Mickey Mouse spot pattern on her side. After her death at 15 years old, a plaque commemorating her service as a "cast member" was installed at Disney's Fort Wilderness Resort and Campground, and her smaller barnyard companions were moved to Disney's Animal Kingdom's Affection Section. The secrecy surrounding her death, even though 15 is quite old for a cow, demonstrates that although people enjoy seeing farm animals and may claim they want to increase their knowledge regarding food production, there are mixed feelings regarding their lifespan, and potentially their uses. (Bir et al. 2019)

Visitors to either SeaWorld Orlando or Walt Disney World expressed higher agreement than nonvisitors that marine and wild mammals can be ethically kept—but lower agreement that livestock can be ethically raised for meat. This sparks questions about self-selection biases and whether seeing animals for entertainment versus consuming them influences attitudes.

Given the widespread interest in travel for entertainment, leisure, and education—often combined into "edutainment" or free-choice learning experiences—so too does the need to engage the public in interactive ways that combine enjoyment with knowledge. Our research seeks to better understand these intersections so that agriculture and food industries can communicate effectively and make sound, data-driven decisions.

WORKS CITED

Bir, Courtney, McKenna Clifford, and Nicole J. Olynk Widmar. 2019. "The Intersection of Manmade 'Natural' Edutainment and Perceptions of Natural Resource Uses." *Environmental Communication.* https://doi.org/10.1080 /17524032.2019.1601634.

Bir, Courtney, Nicole J. Olynk Widmar, and McKenna Clifford. 2020. "The Intersection of 'Natural' Edutainment and Perceptions of Natural Resource Uses." *Environmental Communication* 14, no. 2 168–183.

Adapted from original posting as *ConsumerCorner.2021.Article.03* (https://agribusiness.purdue.edu/consumer_corner/agriculture-and -natural-resources-in-unexpected-places/)

5

WHAT IS DATA, ANYWAY?

E verything is about data these days—data-driven decision making, impassioned arguments about whether public policy decisions are "based on data" or "supported by the data," and so on. But what data are we talking about? Everyone is tossing around *data* as if there is some universally agreed-upon dataset. Soon we'll be calling it *The Data*, using "the" with the same enthusiasm as when referencing The Ohio State University.

Here on *Consumer Corner*, we pride ourselves on being rooted in data-driven insights that can inform sound and timely decision-making. And as an integral aspect of that data-driven approach, we try to be very clear about what data we're referring to, where it came from, who analyzed it, and whether it was peer or otherwise reviewed. It isn't enough to say "the data," and we try to lead by example in being transparent about exactly what data we're using and when.

We've looked at the era of rating one's grocery items in the online marketplace, collected and analyzed data about home gardening from Dr. Courtney Bir, and examined concerns about gluten from Dr. Bailey Norwood (Widmar et al. 2025d, chapter 3). And we've reported on our own peer-reviewed journal articles published using online media data collection and analytics on topics from #Eggs to #USDA to #Disney-World, just to name a few (Widmar et al. 2025c). Closer to home, we dug into the online and public perceptions of Bayer, Dupont, Land O' Lakes, Monsanto, and Syngenta (Widmar et al. 2025c). We've even gone so far as to discuss the (admittedly superior) data-driven decision-making capacity of squirrels (Widmar et al. 2025b, chapter 18).

The core of what happens here rests on data-driven insights, except those few times we ventured into pandemic fashion or the time I called you a hypocrite right to your face and then reminded you to mind your manners (Widmar et al. 2025a). But now, in our fifth book in the series, I think it's time to ask a simple question with a very complicated answer. Much ado about data—but what *is* data, anyway?

According to Dictionary.com, data is "individual facts, statistics, or items of information; information in digital format, as encoded text or numbers, or multimedia images, audio, or video; a body of facts; information" (dictionary.com, 2025). Data stored or encoded as text or numbers is likely the most familiar form, as referenced in a dataset that we might use for quantitative analyses. Qualitative data, often appearing in narrative form—or simply words stored in a variety of formats—results from efforts such as focus groups and interviews and can be analyzed in a variety of ways to derive insights.

Increasingly, we are awash in data, but seldom do we stop to reflect on what data actually *is*. Interestingly, you generate a ton of it yourself. Smart devices in your house, including your TV, your fridge, and other appliances, generate enormous amounts of data. When you include your iPads, iPhones, computers, and those of your family members, your humble household existence is actually a data-generating marvel.

You don't just generate data on what you watch, whom you call and when you do it, what you type, what you buy, and your utility usage (including when). You also generate photos, which contain data including where and at what time those images were captured. Images are data in the image itself, in addition to the data about the image. Videos of your kids (or your cats) are data; that data is usable by a skilled researcher in studying human interactions, but the video itself is also interesting in terms of where it was recorded, by whom, at what time, how you saved it, and whether or not you shared it. Numbers, images, videos, text as data . . . the list goes on, and the forms and scope of what is data is much more varied and diverse than we tend to acknowledge.

WORKS CITED

dictionary.com. (2025). *Data*. Retrieved from dictionary.com/browse: https://www.dictionary.com/browse/data

Widmar, N. J. O., Smith, M. L., & Robinson, E. (2025a). *Consumer Corner: Consumer Lessons From a Pandemic*. Purdue University Press.

Widmar, N. J. O., Smith, M. L., & Robinson, E. (2025b). *Consumer Corner: Decisions That Shape Supply Chains*. Purdue University Press.

Widmar, N. J. O., Smith, M. L., & Robinson, E. (2025c). *Consumer Corner: Market Signals From Online Behavior*. Purdue University Press.

Widmar, N. J. O., Smith, M. L., & Robinson, E. (2025d). *Consumer Corner: Markets We Thought We Knew*. Purdue University Press.

Adapted from original posting as *ConsumerCorner.2021.Letter.15* (https://agribusiness.purdue.edu/consumer_corner/thats-a-wrap-on -2021-in-consumer-corner/)

6

HAVE YOU HUGGED YOUR IPHONE TODAY?

Have you hugged your iPhone today? Silly question, because of course you have. In fact, your iPhone was the last *thing* you saw before you fell asleep and the first *thing* you saw when you woke up. You may have even slept clutching the thing . . . but, hey, I'm not judging. The bottom line is that everything is on that phone. It's really misnamed at this point since you seldom use it to actually make calls, but it does hold the keys to your life from financials to countless modes of communication (especially during COVID-era adaptations when everything about our life is somehow based online; Widmar and Lai 2020).

We in agriculture seem to argue a lot about data privacy issues. I'm guilty of repeating in class, in seminars, and in general conversation my own concern—that while we're busy arguing about who owns the data, someone else is getting busy figuring out how to actually use it (for what it's worth, my bet is on the people working hard on use over those debating ownership of the raw input every time).

Commonly heard in agricultural circles are comments like, "But it's my data!" and "I'm not sharing my data!" But in reality, the vast majority of us are very "cheap dates" in regard to sharing our personal data, so to speak.

If we're really honest, the cat is mostly out of the bag here in the data argument, and it isn't going back in. It doesn't take much in the way of value creation before we're clicking "I agree" on app and software user agreements, generating data galore, and sharing it freely.

Everyone wants to hate Facebook; we point fingers and make faces about its supposed "misuse" of our personal data. But if you aren't paying for the service (your Facebook account is indeed free), then you have to realize that you are the product being sold. That's simply true. And you agreed to it—it was in the terms of service. This wasn't some elaborate scheme played out behind your back (or mine). We willingly post photos of ourselves and our kids, probably without protecting the location or the time the photo was taken, which is a massive privacy issue that we all simply ignore. We willingly share data galore, seemingly because what we get in exchange—the product or service that is the result of the use of that data—is deemed valuable enough to us to make it worthwhile to share.

How does your iPhone know how many minutes you are from home? Actually, how did it even know you were heading toward home as you pulled out of the parking lot at work? Not only did iPhone know where you wanted to go, but it also knew how long it would take to get there. And so you smiled back at iPhone lovingly because it knows you oh so well ... actually, it was Apple Watch you smiled at. Apple Watch, with the brains and memory of the iPhone plus your pulse rate and other fun biological data, but that's a subject for another time.

Back to the agricultural industry's core question again: Why are you so worried about protecting your data? Why aren't you more worried about how to use it? Simply some food for thought. Now, go check your iPhone.

WORK CITED

Widmar, Nicole J. Olynk, and John Lai. 2020. "Internet 'Have Nots' (Including Many Children) Are Suffering Digital Divide Consequences in the COVID-19 Era." *Consumer Corner.* November 2. https://agribusiness.purdue

.edu/consumer_corner/internet-have-nots-are-suffering-digital-divid
-consequences-in-the-covid-19-era/.

———————————

Adapted from original posting as *ConsumerCorner.2021.Letter.17*
(https://agribusiness.purdue.edu/consumer_corner/have-you-hugged
-your-iphone-today/)

7

WE EAT OYSTERS, SO WHY NOT CRICKETS?

BY F. BAILEY NORWOOD AND MELISSA REED

A s the periodical cicadas emerged from the soils of the northeastern United States after their seventeenth year underground, some people came to observe, some came to study, and some came to eat. Recipes were shared online, eating experiments were conducted, and at least one restaurant started serving cicadas in tacos (and soon encountered a run-in with the health department!). Entomophagy (the eating of insects) is a rarity in today's United States, but the recent interest in cicadas suggests attitudes may be changing.

Was this just an anomaly, or do insects have a real chance at establishing a stable market share in the food system? We addressed this question by surveying more than 1,000 Americans to gauge their willingness to consume cookies and shakes made from cricket powder. While insects may currently possess a "yuck" factor, a number of other foods with the potential for disgust have overcome the hurdle and become standard fare. Take oysters, for example, whose appearance and texture resemble a giant ball of snot!

Our survey (Reed et al. 2021) deliberately juxtaposed the "yucky" side of oysters (a standard food) with insect-based foods and then asked individuals about their willingness to consume shakes and cookies made from cricket powder. In other words, we said: "Consider how ordinary these cookies made from crickets look, and consider also the fact that oysters, a regularly consumed food item, resemble mucus. How likely are you to consume oysters and crickets now?" This provides a snapshot of how Americans might view insect-based foods once it is acknowledged that people already consume products with the potential to generate disgust.

A survey of 1,021 Americans probed interest in cricket-flour cookies, finding that among those who have never consumed insect-based food, 37 percent would try it once and 36 percent would eat it on a regular basis if the item is both tasty and safe. When the same survey asked about a cricket-flour milkshake, 36 percent reported they would try it once and 32 percent would eat it on a regular basis if the item is both tasty and safe.

Yet among that same group of respondents, 63 percent would try oysters, but among those who never ate oysters, only 17 percent would try them. Among those who have had oysters, 88 percent indicated they would try them again. Additionally, 52 percent of the same group reported they would eat oysters on a regular basis (10 percent of those who had never tried them and 71 percent of those who had).

The takeaway is this: If oysters can become a regularly consumed food item in the United States, so can crickets!

WORK CITED

Reed, Melissa, F. Bailey Norwood, Wyatt W. Hoback, and Angel Riggs. 2021. "A Survey of Willingness to Consume Insects and a Measure of College Student Perceptions of Insect Consumption Using Q Methodology." *Future Foods* Volume 4, 100046.

Adapted from original posting as *ConsumerCorner.2021.Letter.22* (https://agribusiness.purdue.edu/consumer_corner/we-eat-oysters-so -why-not-crickets/)

8

BREAKING NEWS

People Like Tasty Food—No, Really

BY JEFFREY S. YOUNG

I f I described this article as something like *datalicious*, would that be in poor taste? Sorry for the pun; I'll try to make the rest of this piece more palatable.

People liking things that taste good seems obvious, but it's actually something that too frequently gets assumed by folks interested in studying diets and health. Offended by this seemingly obvious oversight, I set out to measure food tastiness. There were obvious starting points such as "more sugar = more tasty" and "more vitamins = raw veggies = not so tasty," but I wanted something more.

How does an additional gram of sugar impact tastiness? How about sodium? There had to be a way to get more granular with it. As I'll detail below, I managed to pull it off in my peer-reviewed article in *Food Policy* (Young 2021). But so what? What does my formula bring to the table (pardon another food pun)?

Who cares? For one, food marketers care. Sure, they watch for patterns of behavior and demand as they emerge, but what if they could predict those patterns ahead of time—before the competition and before restrictive legislation or new consumption taxes?

The chief audience for the article was food policy researchers. Nearly all of the work I've seen on the favorite "tax junk food, subsidize vegetables" movement looks at sugar-sweetened beverages (SSB) and some mysterious portfolio of fresh fruits and vegetables (FV). The abbreviations "SSB" and "FV" seem to be everywhere if you want to read anything at all on the matter. But that is not how real people eat . . . a little bit of SSB and a whole lot of FV, anyone?

This tastiness formula is the first of its kind. How do I know that? I caught equal amounts of criticism and laughter when I first unveiled it, and I also compulsively checked for anybody having tried to do something like this before and came up empty-handed every time.

Now for that equation: Tastiness for a given food item can be computed as a combination of the nutrient levels per 100g of the food:

$$
\begin{aligned}
Tastiness = {}& 8.82 + 4.43 \ (added\ sugar) + 0.10 \ (sodium) \\
& + 11.27 \ (saturated\ fat) - 8.74 \ (moisture) - 0.64 \ (vitamin\ C) \\
& - 0.06 \ (vitamin\ A) - 0.17 \ (vitamin\ K) - 0.12 \ (calcium) \\
& - 9.63 \ (M.\ unsaturated\ fat) - 8.17 \ (P.\ unsaturated\ fat) \\
& - 12.43 \ (protein) + 0.67 \ (caffeine) - 8.99 \ (carbs) \\
& - 0.23 \ (choline) - 1.05 \ (magnesium) - 1.88 \ (natural\ sugar)
\end{aligned}
$$

If someone wants to run the formula themselves and see how the end results stack up against their own personal taste system, I invite them to do so! There's also a list of more than 150 foods listed in the appendix to the article if you don't feel like doing the math *from scratch* (cooking pun intended).

Others have stated confidently that "taste is random" and should just be assumed away. One paper, which is coauthored by my major professor and very dear mentor, claimed just that. The claim was essentially that we can neither observe nor measure taste, but we can qualitatively look at consumers' diets. One of my favorite quotes from that paper is:

> While someone choosing bran flakes for breakfast may do it strictly for the taste, it is unlikely anyone chooses chocolate-coated sugar bombs for nutrition. In other words, purchasing bran flakes may not be a highly accurate indicator of a demand for nutrition, but purchasing sugar bombs is a good indicator of its absence. (Binkley and Golub 2010)

That is one satisfying mic-drop of an excerpt, at least to me. But it gets at something most people miss: Suppose the people buying the chocolate-coated sugar bombs really are doing so in the full knowledge that they aren't exactly healthy. Reasonable enough, right? So why are they buying them? Are they cheaper than the bran flakes? Certainly not the last time I checked! Do they store better? Doubtful. Are they easier to prepare—that is, pour into a bowl of milk? I would wager not. Where does that leave us? Well, they must taste better, pure and simple.

Find some proxy cereals the next time you grocery shop and look at the leading nutrients for these two competitors. I suspect you'll find a showdown for something like fiber versus sugar. One certainly tastes better than the other in its own right (we don't add pure fiber to our coffee or sprinkle it on grapefruit to improve the taste). What if there were other nutrients like this—some that add to and some that detract from taste? Well, I figured the best way to answer such a question was to get data on folks who (1) tell us their valuations of tastiness and healthiness when considering foods to eat and (2) told us what they ate.

I wrote a computer program to answer the question: Do consumers who prioritize taste over nutrition eat more sugar? Salt? Fat? Protein? Fiber? Vitamin K? You get the idea. And it turns out, yes. Sugar, sodium, and the like were consumed in significantly higher quantities (per total grams of food eaten over a two-day period) by these people, whereas calcium and various vitamins were consumed significantly less. The opposite was true for consumers who prioritized nutrition over taste.

After that comes a bit of black magic, but in short, the relationship between taste-prioritization and the informed—or "data-driven"—list of nutrients can be projected from human beings onto individual food items.

For instance, because adults identified as taste prioritizers ate more sugar, foods high in sugar should taste better (to the average American) than foods low in sugar. Vice versa for foods high or low in dietary fiber. As for the rest of the nutrients in the equation? Here's a quick shortcut: In the equation, any nutrient with a "+" in front of it was identified as taste enhancing by the algorithm, whereas a nutrient with a "-" in front of it detracts from a food item's palatability.

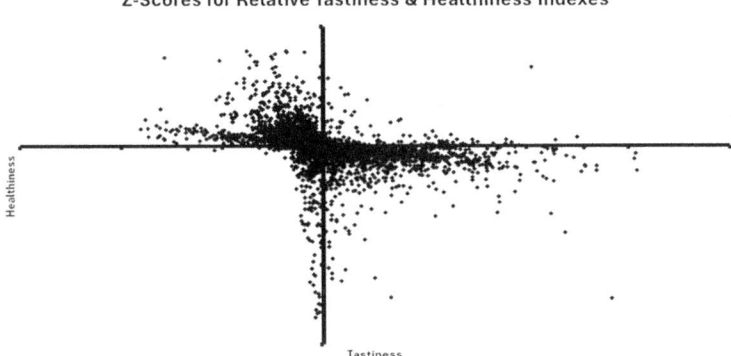

FIGURE 8.1. Visualizing the healthiness-tastiness tension. Graph created by Jeffrey S. Young.

Sure enough, the top-scoring foods in the results include double bacon cheeseburgers and devil's food cake; the bottom of the list has things like raw celery and dry oats. Figure 1 shows the standardized values of the tastiness index and contrasts them with standardized values of a "healthiness" index from another paper written by nutrition researchers.

Makes sense, right? The overwhelming majority of foods eaten by Americans in 2007–2010 were either tasty and bad for you (e.g., deep-dish meat lover's pizza) or healthy and unappealing (e.g., raw watercress). There's a fine line to walk here, but it's not impossible to achieve both—but for what price? That's a story for another time.

The next time somebody says to you, "Well, there's just no accounting for taste," feel free to send them my way! Also, cautiously bear the general, qualitative formula in mind the next time someone appeals to the taste sense as a means of persuasion. After all, we do that all the time with nutritional value. Some common examples: "This has less sugar, so it's healthier," "Oh, good, this one is reduced fat," or "That's a good source of vitamins."

It's also nice to have a tool for reference when thinking about taste. For instance, is the tug-of-war between tastiness and healthfulness of foods a meaningful factor underlying the obesity epidemic in the United States? If so, just how meaningful? This question is briefly addressed in the paper, but it is an increasingly important one for both policymakers and various players in the food industry.

Whatever the case, one thing's for sure: The consumer research world needs more sweet puns. Cantankerous old academics demanding dry, flavorless writing just need to stop being so salty. Okay, now I'm done.

WORKS CITED

Binkley, James K., and Alla Golub. 2010. "Consumer Demand for Nutrition Versus Taste in Four Major Food Categories." *Agricultural Economics.*

Young, Jeffrey. 2021. "Measuring Palatability as a Linear Combination of Nutrient Levels in Food Items." *Food Policy.*

Adapted from original posting as *ConsumerCorner.2021.Letter.31* (https://agribusiness.purdue.edu/consumer_corner/breaking-news -people-like-tasty-food/)

9

BIG DOG DATA IS DRIVING ADVANCEMENTS IN HUMAN HEALTH THROUGH TRANSLATIONAL MEDICINE

BY AUDREY RUPLE

B y studying aging in dogs, we hope to learn how to better match human health span to life span so that we can all live longer, healthier lives," Ruple said (Oates, 2020).

Many opportunities exist in the field of veterinary medical big data where information collected from companion animals, especially dogs, can be used to inform health care decisions in humans. Dogs provide an ideal model for translational medicine as they have the most phenotypic diversity and the greatest number of naturally occurring diseases of all land mammals other than humans. They also share a tremendous amount of ancestral genetic sequence with humans, as well as our physical and chemical environments. The level of sophistication of the health care system for dogs in the United States is second only to that of humans. Thus, data related to dog health presents many opportunities to discover insights into health and disease outcomes in both dog and human populations.

Many veterinary datasets offer advantages over data sources collected in human populations. As we are all well aware now—given ongoing COVID-19-era conversations in nearly every aspect of society—the HIPAA Privacy Act declared medical information, including electronic medical records, protected information. Veterinary patient records, in contrast, are not considered protected health information. Yet our animal companions, especially dogs, share disease outcomes from cancer, eye disorders, and infections (including antimicrobial resistant ones) that can inform human health research. In fact, naturally occurring diseases in companion animals are often similar—and sometimes identical—to human diseases in relation to disease etiology, progression, and response to medical intervention or treatment.

The largest open-access dataset in the United States is part of the Dog Aging Project and includes detailed information about individual dog participants' physical and chemical environments, diet, exercise, behavior, and comprehensive health history (Dog Aging Project, 2024). In a recent open-access journal article, "Veterinary Big Data: When Data Goes to the Dogs," published in *Animals* as part of the special issue "Data-Driven Decision Making in Animal Industries," several veterinary medical datasets well suited for use in translational medicine were described in detail, alongside the advantages and disadvantages of each data source (Paynter et al. 2021).

Datasets from pet hospitals, especially those with hundreds or thousands of clinics that can collect data over a geographically diverse area, offer the opportunity for unique insights. The Veterinary Medical Database (VMDB) is the oldest companion animal health database, providing low-cost or free access to researchers (University of Pretoria, 2023). There are also opportunities from datasets maintained by pet insurance companies, individual research projects, and other ongoing efforts focused on a wide variety of questions in translational and human medicine.

No data source is without limitations, but veterinary medical big data represents an underutilized resource in translational medicine. Employing data from companion animals brought by owners for medical attention may raise fewer ethical concerns than research in which diseases are induced to facilitate their study. The use of medical data collected in dog populations will continue to be a rich source of information that can inform our understanding of both dog and human health, longevity, and disease outcomes. This means that what treatments and medical interventions we, as consumers of human medicine, have available may very well be influenced by data that comes from none other than humankind's long-standing best friend—the dog.

WORKS CITED

Dog Aging Project. (2024). *Discovering the Keys to a Healthy Lifespan.* Retrieved from dogagingproject.org: https://dogagingproject.org/.

Oates, M. (2020, February 4). *Researchers Seek a Helping Paw for Dog Aging Study.* Retrieved from purdue.edu/newsroom: https://www.purdue.edu/newsroom/archive/releases/2020/Q1/researchers-seek-a-helping-paw-for-dog-aging-study.html.

Paynter, A. N., M. D. Dunbar, K. E. Creevy, and A. Ruple. (2021). "Veterinary Big Data: When Data Goes to the Dogs." *Animals*, 11(7).

University of Pretoria. (2023, June 1). *Veterinary Science Open Access Resources: Datasets, Databases and Repositories.* Retrieved from library.up.ac.za: https://library.up.ac.za/c.php?g=1085098&p=7950806.

Adapted from original posting as *ConsumerCorner.2021.Letter.25* (https://agribusiness.purdue.edu/consumer_corner/big-dog-data-is-driving-advancements-in-human-health-through-translational-medicine/)

10

PURPOSEFULLY NOT CONSUMING

Plausible Use of Economics to Understand Minimalism

The concept of consumer behavior is, perhaps, a bit overplayed. Consumer behavior correctly refers to the behavior of a consumer of a service, product, or even information, media, or art. For example, we're all consumers of food and water. While we may not all be consumers of beef, we all consume some sort of calories regularly. But consumer behavior is only one aspect of human behavior. We can behave as consumers seeking to buy or obtain (or consume!) in the marketplace, but many of us also wear other hats and have a variety of other human behaviors—perhaps as producers, sellers, members of the voting public, or agents of societal or cultural change.

The COVID-19 pandemic spurred global economic challenges. As most of us spent increased time at home, a variety of impacts in the marketplace emerged. These impacts ranged from the run on freezers in the summer of 2020 as people sought to store more food, to the inability to find a pool or bike, to entertainment. Home entertainment and home comforts became highly sought after, with different items waxing and waning in popularity seasonally. But all this pandemic shopping occurred alongside a multiyear "less is more" movement toward minimalism.

"The Great Decluttering of 2020: The Pandemic Has Inspired a Clean Out of American Homes" by Jura Koncius in the *Washington Post* depicts people redefining their spaces, creating home offices, repurposing items, or potentially choreographing their home to regain a sense of control over something (Koncius 2020). The pandemic aspect may be somewhat nuanced, but the purging, cleaning out, getting rid of, and repurposing movement is not new. Marie Kondō's book *The Life Changing Magic of Tidying Up* and her Netflix series *Tidying Up With Marie Kondo* were popular before the pandemic (Kondō 2014, 2019). Whether or not an item "brings you joy" is now part of common cultural understanding. If you are not sure what it means to have to touch an item, evaluate whether it sparks joy, and thank it, then you may be missing other recent cultural nuances as well.

Additionally, the Minimalists have been widely featured and are broadly appealing in their promotion of focusing on what matters rather than what does not matter (the minimalists 2025). As an economist who fully appreciates that we all come to the marketplace with differing tastes and preferences, I appreciate their honesty surrounding the struggles of decision-making—including the idea that you must know what you want. Recall from chapter 12 of *The Decisions That Shape Supply Chains* (Widmar et al. 2025):

> Unfortunate Truth One: [about data-driven decision making is that] data can't assist you in making a decision toward an end that you have not yet defined. You have to know where you want to go before you can hope to make decisions that get you there.

"Minimalist Finances and Budgeting" by Joshua Fields Millburn covers a variety of topics surrounding income streams and expenses, most of which are personal decisions that involve trade-offs weighed against individual values, goals, and interests (Millburn 2011). He also presents a universal concept of trade-offs in a way that I think is easily internalized, especially given where we were in 2021 societally. Millburn said, "One principal I live by is questioning all my purchases. It takes time to earn money, and my time is my freedom, so by giving up my money I'm giving up small pieces of my freedom. Before I make a purchase (even for a cup of coffee) I say to myself, 'Is this cup of coffee worth $2 of my freedom?' This has significantly changed my mindset" (Millburn 2011).

The (possible) appeal of minimalism in 2021, from one economist's perspective:

> Changes in consuming, shopping, saving, reusing, keeping and hoarding can all be folded into what is commonly called consumer behavior. Although, upon reflection, it might be more accurate to relabel these actions as "changes in household economics decision making" or "changes in home economics," as not all changes are surrounding consumption—in fact, some are aptly devoted to the lack thereof. (Widmar 2021)

Considering human behavior broadly defined, consumption is only one aspect; leisure, conscious reduction of consumption, or even creation and production are others. The universal concept here lies in trade-offs: To buy is simply to give up money (also measurable in time spent earning the equivalent sum) in exchange for something else. To not buy is to forgo obtaining that "something else," which we tend to assume makes us less happy when we do not have it. But taken at face value, minimalism is about focusing on what matters to the exclusion of what does not (an oversimplification, admittedly), and it is entirely possible to be happier without something or even by giving something away and no longer possessing it. In other words, does the lack of "stuff" in my possession—with or without saving resources (money)—make me happier? It seems that the cost or trade-off of resources, both time and money, to get more stuff is increasingly not worth it to many people.

The law of diminishing marginal utility in economics states that the additional utility we gain from the next unit of consumption declines as we consume more and more units. Is minimalism simply the result of no longer gaining any additional utility or happiness from additional items when we already have so many? Or is managing one's consumption, spending, or resources an activity from which some of us gain additional happiness? Minimalism is popular, and as a mindset, it may offer insights or frameworks for decision-making that make us happier. Diminishing marginal utility is not new, but understanding more about how consumers are making decisions today—and what drives them to consume or not—is helpful in framing our own production, savings, and consumption decisions. It's complicated.

WORKS CITED

Koncius, Jura. 2020. "The Great Decluttering of 2020: The Pandemic Has Inspired a Cleanout of American Homes." *The Washington Post.* August 5. https://www.washingtonpost.com/lifestyle/home/the-big-pandemic-clean-out-clearing-the-junk-out-of-your-home-while-stuck-there/2020/08/04/230d71d2-c868-11ea-a99f-3bbdffb1af38_story.html.

Kondō, Marie. 2014. *The Life-Changing Magic of Tidying Up: The Japanese Art of Decluttering and Organizing.* Ten Speed Press.

Kondō, Marie. 2019. *Tidying Up with Marie Kondo.* Directed by Jade Sandberg Wallis. Performed by Marie Kondō.

Millburn, Joshua Fields. 2011. "Minimalist Finances and Budgeting." theminimalists.com/finances. https://www.theminimalists.com/finances/.

the minimalists. 2025. "theminimalists.com." theminimalists.com. https://www.theminimalists.com/.

Widmar, Nicole J. Olynk. 2021. "COVID-19 Consumer Behavior Contributions: June 2020–July 2021 Summary." *Consumer Corner.* July 16. https://agribusiness.purdue.edu/consumer_corner/covid-19-consumer-behavior-contributions-june-2020-july-2021/.

Widmar, Nicole J. Olynk, Michael L. Smith, and Erin Robinson. 2025. *Consumer Corner: Decisions That Shape Supply Chains.* Purdue University Press.

Adapted from original posting as *ConsumerCorner.2021.Letter.29* (https://agribusiness.purdue.edu/consumer_corner/pusposefully-not-consuming-plausible-use-of-economics-to-understand-minimalism/)

11

GETTING TO THE WHY BEHIND CONSUMERS' DECISIONS

How Qualitative Data Can Help

BY BRENNA ELLISON

The world is awash in data, but what is data? Datasets comprised of numeric entries get much of the attention in economics, yet, as we covered in chapter 3, there is more to data than numbers and more than one methodology to employ. Qualitative data, which are often derived from focus groups and interviews, can be an important complement to more traditional quantitative sources of data like surveys, scanner, and sales data.

To illustrate the value of qualitative data, consider an example related to food pantries on college campuses. You may have noticed stories in the news on college students going hungry, with some studies estimating nearly 40 percent of students experience food insecurity (Laterman 2019; Hope4College 2020; Ellison et al. 2021). In response, many college campuses have established food pantries for students; however, survey research suggests food pantry use is low relative to the proportion of students who report experiencing food insecurity (Swipe Out Hunger 2025; McArthur et al. 2020).

If researchers relied solely on quantitative data from surveys and concluded that (1) food insecurity is high on campus and (2) food pantry use is low, a natural response might be to increase awareness of the food pantry among students—in other words, more education and more marketing. However, qualitative inquiry can help us dig deeper to understand *why* food-insecure students are not using this resource. In our own research, we found that students believed food pantries were "for real poor people," even though some were experiencing dire food situations themselves (Nikolaus et al. 2019). Other researchers interviewed students and also concluded that there is a real stigma around using food pantries among college students (El Zein et al. 2018). Thus, the recommendation to simply improve awareness would likely do little to improve pantry use.

So, what are the takeaways here? First, numeric data can tell us a lot, but rarely do they tell us everything. Qualitative data can serve as an important complement for understanding the *why* behind consumers' decisions. You might think that we can just ask consumers why they behave in a certain way on surveys, but that assumes (1) we know the appropriate answer choices to give them and (2) consumers are able and willing to articulate the reason(s) for their behavior. Human beings' optimal choices may change depending on the choice set presented or be otherwise context-dependent, making the articulation of reasons a challenge in many settings. Qualitative inquiry allows researchers to have a conversation with consumers and offers space for additional probing when answers are unclear or suggest something more is at play.

Second, words matter (Widmar et al. 2025, chapter 5). In the food pantry example, more education and marketing are unlikely to remove the stigma associated with using this resource among college students. But do we have to call it a food pantry? Perhaps a better path forward is to reframe—or even rename—the resource, which is exactly what happened at my former institution. The University of Illinois launched its Food Assistance and Well-Being Program in 2020 and found much higher rates of use among students compared to a more traditional food pantry on campus.

WORKS CITED

Ellison, B., Bruening, M., Hruschka, D. J., Nikolaus, C. J., van Woerden, I., Rabbitt, M. P., and Nickols-Richardson, S. M. (2021). "Viewpoint: Food Insecurity Among College Students: A Case for Consistent and Comparable Measurement." *Food Policy*, 101.

El Zein, A., Mathews, A. E., House, L., & Shelnutt, K. P. (2018). "Why Are Hungry College Students Not Seeking Help? Predictors of and Barriers to Using an On-Campus Food Pantry." *Nutrients*, 10(9).

Hope4College. (2020). *#RealCollege 2020: Five Years of Evidence on Basic Needs Insecurity.* Retrieved from hope4college.com: https://hope4college.com /realcollege-2020-five-years-of-evidence-on-basic-needs-insecurity/.

Laterman, K. (2019, May 2). "Tuition or Dinner? Nearly Half of College Students Surveyed in a New Report Are Going Hungry." *The New York Times*. Retrieved from https://www.nytimes.com/2019/05/02/nyregion/hunger-college-food -insecurity.html.

McArthur, L. H., Fasczewski, K. S., Farris, A. R., & Petrone, M. (2020). "Use and Perceptions of a Campus Food Pantry Among Food Insecure College Students." *Journal of Appalachian Health*, 2, no. 2.

Nikolaus, C. J., Ellison, B., & Nickols-Richardson, S. M. (2019). "College Students' Interpretations of Food Security Questions: Results from Cognitive Interviews." *BMC Public Health*, 19, 1282.

Swipe Out Hunger. (2025). *Welcome to Swipe Out Hunger.* Retrieved from https:// swipehunger.org/: https://swipehunger.org/aboutus/.

Widmar, N. J. O., M. L. Smith, and E. Robinson. (2025). *Consumer Corner: Decisions That Shape Supply Chains.* Purdue University Press.

Adapted from original posting as *ConsumerCorner.2021.Letter.32* (https://agribusiness.purdue.edu/consumer_corner/getting-to-the-why -behind-consumers-decisions/)

12

I KNOW SOMETHING YOU DON'T KNOW

A t Consumer Corner, we are all about data, including from non-traditional sources. In chapter 4 of the first book in our *Consumer Corner* series, *Decisions That Shape Supply Chains* by Widmar, Smith, and Robinson (2025), we proposed:

> Transparency and honesty are good . . . but forcing consumers to confront uncomfortable truths is essentially ripping off Mickey's gloves to reveal the rodent paws underneath. If consumers are asking questions, providing truthful information about agricultural production is the right response; however, be sensitive to the fact that what we share could be perceived negatively by others. Answer the call for transparency, but don't rip off Mickey's gloves without warning.

What we are really saying here is that we should share information because people want access to it, or because they have asked for it. Sharing information with people because we, the sharer, want to impose or force information on someone else can be perceived negatively (and for good reason).

Indeed, caution may be warranted in how we respond to consumer requests for information, or how we might wish to forcibly provide unrequested information. However, more fundamental market information and data in food and agricultural industries has generally been considered public data in the United States. In an article in *Choices* magazine entitled, "'Big Data' Provides Insights to Public Perceptions of USDA," we outlined how information asymmetries are a near-universally accepted contributing factor toward market failures and documented the roles of public information from the United States Department of Agriculture (USDA) and associated agencies in building and sustaining US agricultural and food markets (Widmar 2019).

Agricultural and applied economists have studied information asymmetry of agricultural markets for inputs and outputs, as well as extensively in food markets. Historically, a cornerstone of US agricultural industries has been investments to lessen the impacts of information asymmetries through the creation of information sources in the public domain (Widmar 2019). Essentially, the United States has long (and heavily) invested in creating information that serves as a public good in food and agriculture (Widmar 2019). The USDA provides leadership on food, agriculture, natural resources, rural development, nutrition, and related issues based on public policy, the best available science, and effective management (USDA 2019a). The USDA states:

> We have a vision to provide economic opportunity through innovation, helping rural America to thrive; to promote agriculture production that better nourishes Americans while also helping feed others throughout the world; and to preserve our Nation's natural resources through conservation, restored forests, improved watersheds, and healthy private working lands. (USDA, 2019a)

Widmar (2019) details the USDA's and affiliated agencies' roles and developments as follows:

> The USDA and its affiliated agencies provide data and reporting that is universally accessible and employed by firms, farms, and agencies to

make decisions. The National Institute of Food and Agriculture (NIFA) is a federal agency within the USDA that is part of USDA's Research, Education, and Economics (REE) mission area (USDA, 2019d). The mission of the USDA's Economic Research Service (ERS) is "to anticipate trends and emerging issues in agriculture, food, the environment, and rural America and to conduct high-quality, objective economic research to inform and enhance public and private decision making" (USDA 2019b). The USDA's National Agricultural Statistics Service (NASS) conducts surveys every year to inform reports on virtually every aspect of U.S. agriculture (USDA, 2019c). Production, price, market, labor, finance, and agri-supply chain data (including on-farm labor and wages) are some examples of data and reporting by NASS, which "report[s] the facts on American agriculture, facts needed by people working in and depending upon U.S. agriculture" and "provide[s] objective and unbiased statistics on a preannounced schedule that is fair and impartial to all market participants," among other endeavors (USDA 2019c).

The sheer volume of media coverage following a much-anticipated USDA report release is evidence of the importance of this information in the marketplace. Correspondents and market analysts need not agree with the information provided; entire publications exist to debate the USDA's reports and predictions. Nonetheless, even those who offer counterarguments and commentary would not be able to do so without a public information source. In most cases, only the largest or best-funded companies could acquire data and analytics; the USDA puts this information into the public domain. The precise estimates provided in news releases and reports aside, the fundamental value of public information from the USDA and associated agencies remains a cornerstone of US agriculture and food markets.

US Secretary of Agriculture Sonny Perdue announced on August 9, 2018, that further reorganization of the USDA was to take place (USDA 2018). The ERS, which was under the REE mission area, was to realign with the Office of the Chief Economist (OCE) under the Office of the Secretary, and most employees of the ERS and NIFA were to be relocated outside the Washington, DC region. Movement of employees and the agency was expected to be completed by the end of December 2019. The relocation fueled a national debate, with 294 of 315 NIFA staff and 253 of 329 ERS staff told to uproot and move or leave (Bach 2019).

While 2020 through 2022 saw continued challenges in public policy surrounding the ongoing pandemic, we also anticipated uncertainty in agricultural trade relationships, antitrust debates heightening in meat markets, and all of the "normal" discussions about costs of production, weather, and more (Thompson 2022; Abbott 2022). Correspondents may argue and market specialists will continue to disagree, but the fact that we have data and market summaries to disagree with and argue about is incredibly valuable.

In a world where we continue to struggle to find any consensus, let's ensure that we value the public data in agricultural and food markets that enables our agricultural businesses to move forward. And remember: Progress does not require consensus, which is good—because I don't see consensus on the horizon. Still, our agricultural industries have gotten quite adept at progress in an uncertain environment (Widmar 2020a). We said it back in 2022 on *Consumer Corner*, but it's worth remembering what we learned at the end of 2020: "Trying to Help When, Where, and How We're Able" (Widmar 2020b):

> When I was a little boy and something bad happened in the news, my mother would tell me to look for the helpers. You'll always find people helping, she'd say. And I've found that that's true. In fact, it's one of the best things about our wonderful world. (Rogers 1983)

WORKS CITED

Abbott, Chuck. 2022. "U.S. Will Vigorously Enforce Fair-Play Laws in Meatpacking, Says Biden." *Successful Farming*. January 4. https://www.agriculture.com/news/business/us-will-vigorously-enforce-fair-play-laws-in-meatpacking-says-biden.

Bach, N. 2019. "USDA Faces Exodus of Scientists as Employees Are Forced to Move to Kansas City." Fortune.com. Available online: https://fortune.com /2019/07/17/usda-employees-kansas-city-relocation/ [Accessed 10/30/ 2019].

Rogers, Fred. 1983. *Look for the Helpers* PSA 2001. Performed by Fred Rogers. https://www.misterrogers.org/videos/look-for-the-helpers.

Thompson, Bill. 2022. "US Ag Faces International Uncertainty in 2022." agri -pulse.com. January 5. https://www.agri-pulse.com/articles/17004-us-ag-faces -international-uncertainty-in-2022.

US Department of Agriculture. 2018. "USDA to Realign ERS with Chief Economist, Relocate ERS & NIFA Outside DC." Washington, DC: U.S. Department of Agriculture, Press Release 0162.18.

US Department of Agriculture. 2019a. *About USDA.* US Department of Agriculture. Available online: https://www.usda.gov/our-agency/about -usda [Accessed 10/30/2019].

US Department of Agriculture. 2019b. *About ERS.* US Department of Agriculture, Economic Research Service. Available online: https://www.ers.usda.gov /about-ers/ [Accessed 10/30/2019].

US Department of Agriculture. 2019c. *About NASS.* US Department of Agriculture, National Agricultural Statistics Service. Available online: https://www .nass.usda.gov/About_NASS/index.php [Accessed 10/30/2019].

US Department of Agriculture. 2019d. *About NIFA.* US Department of Agriculture, National Institute of Food and Agriculture. Available online: https://nifa .usda.gov/about-nifa [Accessed 10/30/2019].

Widmar, Nicole J. Olynk. 2019. "'Big Data' Provides Insights to Public Perceptions of USDA." *Choices.* Quarter 4. Available online: http://www.choicesmagazine .org/choices-magazine/submitted-articles/big-data-provides-insights-to -public-perceptions-of-usda.

Widmar, Nicole J. Olynk. 2020a. "Progress Is Required; Consensus Is Not." purdue.edu/consumer_corner. December 14. https://agribusiness.purdue.edu /consumer_corner/progress-is-required-consensus-is-not/.

Widmar, Nicole J. Olynk. 2020b. "Trying to Help When, Where and How We're Able." *Consumer Corner.* December 8. https://agribusiness.purdue.edu /consumer_corner/trying-to-help/.

Widmar, Nicole J. Olynk, Michael L. Smith, and Erin Robinson. 2025. *Consumer Corner: Decisions That Shape Supply Chains.* Purdue University Press.

Adapted from original posting as *ConsumerCorner.2022.Letter.1* (https://www.agribusiness.purdue.edu/consumer_corner/i-know -something-you-dont-know/)

13

CHILDCARE APPS—
FRIEND OR FOE?

BY BRENNA ELLISON

think most parents agree—finding childcare is stressful! Parents have long served as our example of stressed-out consumers on *Consumer Corner* (Widmar et al. 2025, chapter 2). Millions of US parents require care for their young children. The National Center for Education Statistics estimates that 59 percent of children age five and under receive nonparental childcare at least once per week (NCES 2021). Not only do parents have to find childcare, they also have to find affordable care from a provider they trust—no easy task.

For parents who use childcare centers, mobile apps such as Brightwheel, Kangarootime, and HiMama are increasingly common tools for managing communication between parents and childcare providers. These apps provide an in-depth look at a child's day: when they eat, nap (if you're lucky!), and go to the bathroom; when incidents occur, and so on. They also send updates or announcements about class parties, school closures, and the like. And, of course, the provider can share pictures—mostly cute, though an occasional picture of a rash or bite mark may sneak in.

While the apps are marketed as improving efficiency and accountability for childcare providers, they are clearly designed to offer transparency for parents who want assurance that their child is safe and appropriately cared for. I, too, want a good environment for my children when I cannot be with them. But is it possible these apps create data and information overload for parents? And it isn't just numerical data we're being bombarded with. Recall from chapter 5 ("What Is Data, Anyway?") that we're talking words, pictures, and videos.

For example, a few weeks ago, I received several messages about my one-year-old from his classroom, in addition to the standard updates on eating and napping:

- 9:16 a.m.: Diaper, wet and BM; massive blowout—please bring more clothes for the cubby!
- 4:01 p.m.: Incident: [Child's name] was in a friend's personal space, and the friend happened to bite. We separated them immediately and iced [child's] arm. He was feeling better in a couple of minutes.

Reminder: This is *one* day. As the mom, I'm thinking a few things:

1. I have gross clothes to clean at home tonight . . . ugh.
2. Did they really need to tell me it was a blowout? And did I need that information immediately? This feels like a "need-to-know" issue paired with a timing question. An end-of-day surprise might have been better than a day full of dread.
3. He got bit *again* (and, terribly, in the back of my mind—will he ever bite back? Should he?).
4. And about the biting: Why do we call the other child a "friend"? A small part of me says (to myself, of course), "I don't think 'friend' is the right term. Friends don't chew on friends . . . do they?"

On days like this, I'm also feeling a bit (okay, a lot) guilty. After all, what kind of mom knows their child is having a rough day and doesn't pick him up early?

I suspect I'm not the only parent who has experienced this wide range of emotions from real-time data delivered via a childcare app. Anecdotally, I know several parents who, like me, dread those notifications. The thought crosses their minds: *Please don't let it be a school closure or a high fever.*

So what are parents to do? While the information stream is unlikely to stop, it is possible to slow it down. Parents can adjust their notification settings so their phones aren't buzzing all day. And while the process of turning off notifications may cause some guilt, information overload is a real thing—as is the anxiety that comes with it. There doesn't seem to be a right answer or single solution. Which leads to the next question: Is it possible that the cutesy, easy-to-use, adorable childcare app—the portal from parent to child every day—is actually presenting the parenting equivalent of a wicked problem, where sometimes all the data is simply too much?

Will more frequent notifications cause you to change your childcare situation? Likely not; childcare can be very difficult to find and important to maintain. But you may be less attentive to your own responsibilities during the day, while carrying that aforementioned guilt— which may bring its own set of consequences.

WORKS CITED

NCES. 2021. "Fast Facts on Child Care." nces.ed.gov/fastfacts. https://nces.ed.gov/fastfacts/display.asp?id=4.

Widmar, Nicole J. Olynk, Michael L. Smith, and Erin Robinson. 2025. *Consumer Corner: Decisions That Shape Supply Chains.* Purdue University Press.

Adapted from original posting as *ConsumerCorner.2023.Letter.11* (https://agribusiness.purdue.edu/consumer_corner/childcare-apps-friend-or-foe/)

14

WELL, YOU'RE ALSO A LIAR

BY NICOLE J. OLYNK WIDMAR AND COURTNEY BIR

I n Book One in the *Consumer Corner* series, we talked about how you were (almost certainly, well, definitely) a hypocrite (Widmar et al. 2025, chapter 3). That's still the case (sorry to be the one to tell you). In the same book, we also addressed YouTube-worthy temper tantrums and why they need to stop, and we finished with some tough-love recognition that you (probably, well . . . almost certainly) deserved that natural consequence the universe so kindly provided (Widmar et al. 2025, chapters 10 and 13).

It's now time to consider whether, on top of being a hypocrite, you're also a liar. Now, "liar" is a rather strong term. Your lying may not be intentional, and it may not even involve other people. Giving you the benefit of the doubt, you may just be unintentionally lying to yourself.

Forgive the jest and the admittedly loose interpretation of our own research, but we're really talking about biases in self-reported data more so than lying, per se. But hopefully you can appreciate the spirit of the conversation, even if we're taking liberties (and grossly insulting you along the way). This discussion is based on the open-access published research paper "Consistently Biased" (Bir and Widmar 2020).

We seek to understand human behavior here on *Consumer Corner*. Most of the time we're looking at how we consume food, goods, services, or even just how we spend our own time. We use various data sources to study consumption, including survey data. But survey data comes with concerns, including a whole assortment of biases. One bias we've studied extensively is social desirability bias (SDB). Most Americans admit—or, more positively stated, report—that they make New Year's resolutions. In fact, we've found 60–63 percent report a resolution to lose weight (Bir and Widmar 2020). With all the healthy holiday chatter about working out, losing weight, and starting the new year off right, one must wonder how accurate the data surrounding these good intentions really is. We wondered the same thing and investigated how social desirability bias might impact self-reported data on these and related holiday behaviors.

SDB occurs due to a subconscious effort to make yourself look better by responding to a question in a "socially correct" way. Consider being asked if you eat healthy. You want to answer "yes" because you want the person asking to think highly of you. "Yes" is the socially better answer, regardless of whether you actually eat well—or even try. Bluntly stated, you simply don't want to answer "no" because it sounds bad. The bottom line is there is a propensity for respondents to underreport bad behaviors and overreport good behaviors.

In fact, overreporting good behavior relative to reporting on the "average person" has been found in a series of our studies—including this chapter—to be unbelievably consistent (Bir and Widmar 2020). To examine the propensity for SDB, we asked respondents about their holiday behaviors, both healthy and unhealthy, in two ways: about their own behaviors and about the behaviors of the average American. This approach works because while people tend to succumb to social pressure when answering about themselves, research shows there is far less social pressure when answering about the average person. In fact, when we answer about the average person, we are likely projecting our own viewpoints, beliefs, and behaviors instead.

The share of respondents exhibiting SDB, reporting themselves in a more favorable light than they reported about the average American, was found to be incredibly consistent. Table 14.1 shows the results. For the statement, "I anticipate gaining weight during the holiday season," the percentage who exhibit SDB was 55 percent, whereas the percentage of

TABLE 14.1. *Percent of Respondents Exhibiting Evidence of SDB (n = 367)*

STATEMENT	% OF RESPONDENTS EXHIBITING EVIDENCE OF SDB
I anticipate gaining weight during the holiday season.	55%
I will gain more weight during the holiday season than during other times of the year.	59%
I make a New Year's resolution to lose weight.	62%
I will maintain my workout schedule during the holiday season.	41%
I will be vigilant about my weight during the holiday season.	30%
I watch what I eat during the holiday season.	35%
I will consume more desserts during the holiday season than at other times of the year.	48%
I will consume more alcohol during the holiday season than at other times of the year.	66%

individuals exhibiting SDB for "I will maintain my workout schedule during the holiday season" was 41 percent.

Across all eight behavioral statements—covering diet, exercise, dessert, and alcohol consumption—an interesting pattern emerges: Respondents reported healthier habits for themselves and more indulgent or unhealthy behaviors when asked the same question about the "average American." In other words, respondents tended to think their lifestyle is slightly better than everyone else's. This is a clear indicator of SDB. After all, only half of us can be above average at anything.

On statements related to weight gain, eating habits, or intentions to exercise, more than half of respondents exhibited signs of SDB. All together, we have a simple takeaway. Even during the holidays when many of us license ourselves to more indulgent behavior, we engage in biased self-appraisal.

We also tested whether a cheap-talk statement—a note reminding respondents of the tendency to misreport and asking them to answer truthfully—would reduce bias. The cheap-talk statement provided to half of the randomly assigned respondents developed for this study was: "Human inclination may be to answer questions in a way that deviates from your true behavior in an effort to improve the impression you make on others. This desire to give what is believed to be the socially 'correct' or acceptable answer is often referred to as social desirability bias. Please keep this inclination in mind and try to reflect on your true behavior when answering questions."

What did we find? Only one of the eight statements showed a significantly lower occurrence of SDB among respondents who saw the cheap-talk statement. Taken together, the incidence of SDB is reasonably high, but not necessarily unexpected given the subject matter (weight, holiday eating and drinking, resolution). More surprising is how consistent people are in rating themselves better than the average person—evidence of SDB in this work. Yes, it is possible for an individual to do more than the average person in good behaviors and fewer bad behaviors than average, but not for all of us. We can't all be above average in both directions, especially considering we ourselves are part of the population we're rating.

Given how much health and medical decision-making relies on self-reported data, the ability to get that data as accurate as possible is critical. When it comes to self-reporting health behaviors, at least around the holidays, it appears most of us are better than average, which is a data problem worth pondering.

WORKS CITED

Bir, Courtney, and Nicole J. Olynk Widmar. 2020. "Consistently Biased: Documented Consistency in Self-Reported Holiday Healthfulness Behaviors and Associated Social Desirability Bias." *Humanities and Social Sciences Communications* 7, article 178. Available at https://www.nature.com/articles/s41599-020-00665-x.

Widmar, Nicole J. Olynk, Michael L. Smith, and Erin Robinson. 2025. *Consumer Corner: Decisions That Shape Supply Chains.* Purdue University Press.

Adapted from original posting as *ConsumerCorner.2022.Article.1* (https://agribusiness.purdue.edu/consumer_corner/well-youre-also-a-liar/)

15

DO YOU TRUST ME?

BY JEFFREY S. YOUNG

I n late 2021, I partnered with *Consumer Corner* on a nationally representative survey of US households to explore a timely (and dare I say . . .
provocative) question about public trust. In particular, we examined
confidence in some of the "big" systems that shape our daily lives.

Trust matters. It influences everything from public response to health
measures during a pandemic (Widmar and Bir 2021) to confidence in financial, governmental, and food systems. Consumers under duress turn
to those they trust to provide stability (Widmar et al. 2025, chapter 2). But
how much do they actually trust the systems in place today? And how
much will they trust them in the future?

We asked respondents to rate their confidence in various institutions on
a scale from 1 (no confidence) to 7 (total confidence). Generally speaking,
the majority view the US military's stability and sustainability very positively, while the opposite is true for the federal government.

Alternatively, we can look for the proportion of the population that
scored a system 5 or higher. That is, what percent of the United States has
a positive view of a given institution or establishment? Those results ap-
pear in Table 2.

Confidence in the military stands out, while federal government and
economic systems receive comparatively low positive ratings. But does geography play a role? Using four US regions in the survey, Northeast, South,
Midwest, and West, we looked at spatial heterogeneity in people's confidence regionally. The patterns are displayed in Table 3.

TABLE 15.1. *Average Confidence in US Systems*

INSTITUTION	AVERAGE SCORE
Financial system	4.04
Food system	4.23
Military	4.9
Federal government	3.63
Higher education	4.24
Tech sector	4.03
Economy	3.68
State government	3.89
Health care system	3.93

Scale: 1 = no confidence, 7 = total confidence

TABLE 15.2. *Proportion of Respondents with Positive Confidence (Scored 5 or Higher)*

INSTITUTION	PERCENT
Financial system	39%
Food system	42%
Military	63%
Federal government	34%
Higher education	44%
Tech sector	38%
Economy	32%
State government	39%
Health care system	38%

Respondents in the West tend to be more optimistic overall, while those in the South report the lowest levels of confidence across most systems. As we continue to analyze these patterns, questions remain: How will trust—or lack thereof—shape consumer behavior? Will confidence in public systems influence future choices about food, health, and financial security? Trust is dynamic, and understanding its role in consumer decision-making will remain essential.

TABLE 15.3. *Proportion of Respondents with a Positive Confidence (Scored 5 or Higher), by Region*

CATEGORY	NORTHEAST	SOUTH	MIDWEST	WEST
Financial system	38.69%	37.14%	38.55%	44.64%
Food system	41.61%	36.43%	45.18%	49.40%
Military	63.50%	59.29%	66.87%	65.48%
Federal government	37.96%	30.00%	27.71%	42.86%
Higher education	49.64%	37.14%	45.78%	48.81%
Tech sector	45.99%	34.64%	36.14%	40.48%
Economy	38.69%	28.57%	30.12%	35.12%
State government	39.42%	34.29%	39.76%	44.64%
Health care system	40.15%	33.93%	38.55%	42.26%

WORKS CITED

Widmar, Nicole J. Olynk, and Courtney Bir. 2021. "Social Values & Mask Wearing in 2020: A Data Visualization." *Consumer Corner.* October 4. https://agribusiness.purdue.edu/consumer_corner/social-values-and-mask-wearing-in-2020-a-data-visualization/.

Widmar, Nicole J. Olynk, Michael L. Smith, and Erin Robinson. 2025. *Consumer Corner: Decisions That Shape Supply Chains.* Purdue University Press.

Adapted from original posting as *ConsumerCorner.2022.Letter.2* (https://agribusiness.purdue.edu/consumer_corner/do-you-trust-me/)

16

WHO'S IN CHARGE
HERE, ANYWAY?

BY JEFFREY S. YOUNG

n chapter 15, we examined public trust in large institutions. Regardless of how much trust exists in the public and private systems, another
question arises: "Who should be in charge of what, and to what degree?"
This "who's in charge here?" question is precisely what we address now.

Debate is ongoing around the US health care system, the protection of
natural resources, regulations on the airline industry, and a bunch of other
public-private tensions. So what is the general opinion on what should
fall under government versus private control?

Table 16.1 summarizes responses. On a scale from 1 (totally private) to
7 (totally public), a median score of 4 represents a perfectly balanced preference between no government intervention and total government control.

Scores above 4 indicate a preference for more government intervention than private control; anything below 4 indicates a preference
for privatization. Scores near 4 suggest either an even split or a hybrid
private-public approach. These average opinions are aggregated and
shown in Table 16.2.

Services averaging above 4 include parks and recreation (fantastic show,
by the way), natural resource management, fire services, domestic police
protection, and the military. Those averaging below 4 include grocery and
food procurement, banking and financial services, and air travel. Education and health-related services fall near 4, suggesting a mixed view.

TABLE 16.1. *Mean Preference for Government vs. Private Control*

SERVICE	MEAN SCORE
Public ground transportation (e.g. bus, train)	4.04
Air travel	3.86
Parks & recreation (bike trails, museums)	4.37
Health, pharmaceutical, and medical services	3.98
Banking and financial services	3.57
Grocery and food procurement services	3.23
Natural resource management	4.41
Education	3.97
Domestic police protection	4.59
Fire services	4.55
Military services	5.22

Scale: 1 = totally private, 7 = totally public; higher scores indicate stronger preference for government management

TABLE 16.2. *Proportion Favoring More Public or More Private Control*

	MORE PRIVATE (RANKING <4)	MORE PUBLIC (RANKING >4)
Grocery and food	53%	25%
Banking and finance	45%	31%
Air travel	39%	37%
Military services	18%	67%
Domestic police	26%	53%
Fire services	26%	51%

A final observation is that polarization skews more toward government than private control. Look at the difference on the "more private" margin. It is +28% for groceries, +14% for banking, and just 2% for air travel. On the "more public" side, the margins are far larger: +49% for military services, +27% for police, and +25% for fire services.

In general, these results tell us that the public may be more dependent on government leadership (or assistance) than we often care to admit. At the very least, average Americans are warming up more to the idea of publicly funded and administrated social amenities than they once may have been.

———————

Adapted from original posting as *ConsumerCorner.2022.Letter.7* (https://agribusiness.purdue.edu/consumer_corner/whos-in-charge-here -anyway/)

17

EVERYTHING
IS JUST MATH

We talk a lot about data-driven decision-making on *Consumer Corner*, because there are many good reasons to use data to make business decisions. The problem is that when we become data-driven, we face a few unfortunate truths, which we explored in great detail in our chapter "Don't Eat Random Mushrooms" from *Decisions That Shape Supply Chains* (Widmar et al. 2025a). You might recall from that chapter that Unfortunate Truth #2 was that if we are going to make data-driven decisions, then we can no longer do whatever we want, what feels right, or what our gut says to do. Instead, we may have to do things we might not necessarily want *to do*.

The House Advantage by Jeffrey Ma outlines a whole series of examples of Unfortunate Truth #2. There is a freely available keynote clip (https://www.youtube.com/watch?v=yKot22nCkuE) *from one of Ma's talks, and the 10 minutes you spend watching it may be the most valuable 10 minutes you* devote to thinking about data-driven decision-making (Ma 2019).

If you're not familiar, Jeff Ma was the real-life inspiration for the movie *21*, gaining worldwide recognition in the MIT Blackjack Club. He used math to beat the house and says, "Every decision you make at that blackjack table is 100% objective; there is no subjectivity, the numbers are all played out. Blackjack was big data before there was even such a thing." *The House Advantage: Playing the Odds to Win Big in Business* (Ma 2010) is required reading in my Farm Management class where I pose the question: How is making a decision in blackjack—a game in which we have probabilities of various outcomes but no certainty—any different from making a decision on the farm where we also have probabilities of various outcomes but no certainty?

In agriculture, we are often guilty of saying, "Ag is different because *x, y, z*." Indeed, we have great debates in my Farm Management class about how agricultural production is unique because it is based in a biological process, making it different from a production line in many ways. Crops and livestock production are biologically governed; you cannot plant a corn crop in Iowa in January. Similarly, you cannot make more chicken wings without making more of all other parts of the chicken (Widmar et al. 2025b, chapter 8).

Quite a bit of the pain felt in meat markets during COVID-19 adjustments stemmed from the fact that certain cuts of the animal were in extremely high demand (those we were cooking and eating at home!), while demand for other cuts fell rapidly due to restaurant closures. Yet the biological process demands that we produce the whole animal. We cannot simply convert a hypothetical production line for hams into one for bacon—we can only produce more pigs.

Agricultural production is biologically governed—and also at the mercy of natural occurrences for water (rain) and energy (weather, sunlight, temperature). That said, the outcomes, though perhaps more variable than in more tightly controllable processes, are still bounded and quantifiable. We know corn yield will not be less than zero. Now, yields may vary widely from year to year, but certainly we can agree they fall between 0 bushels and the record high of 616 bushels per acre (BASF 2019). If you are an optimist expecting to surpass the standing record by a significant margin, then perhaps you would argue for a range of 0 to 800 bushels per acre. That's fine, but what you cannot argue is that the uncertainty makes it impossible to do the math to make a data-driven decision.

Furthermore, while we may not know the exact probabilities of each outcome, we do know more than we often admit. It is less likely to achieve 800 bushels than 267. With historical field data, we could make a fairly educated guess of what yield is more likely than another and assign reasonable probabilities to our expected outcomes.

I would argue that agricultural production is indeed different from traditional manufacturing lines in a variety of ways. Just as blackjack is "simply math" (a set of possible outcomes with probabilities attached), we can make data-driven decisions in agricultural production to a much greater degree than we currently do. Spend enough time engrossed in *The House Advantage* or listening to Jeff Ma's talks, and you will start to see that nearly every decision you make—and nearly everything that "happens" to you—is quantifiable. As we say in class, it really is all just math. Data-driven decision-making is possible and often preferable to relying solely on gut or intuition. It becomes harder over time to find situations that aren't "just math." For example, health decisions and treatment choices can be framed in terms of recovery probabilities, and fertilizer application rates can be approached by analyzing likely yield outcomes under various weather conditions.

The bottom line is that while we talk a lot about data-driven decision-making, we often fall back on excuses about why our incredibly unique situations require intuition instead of math. I am sure there are cases where this might be true, but is that because the process truly cannot be quantified, or because we would rather avoid parameterizing the problem, making our assumptions transparent, and facing what the math recommends? More commonly, perhaps, the data-driven answer points to something we simply don't want to do.

Taking inspiration from Jeff Ma's book . . . imagine you are Ma, sitting at the blackjack table, counting cards. You know the mathematically correct move, but the last time you made it, you lost. That doesn't matter—the decision was still correct because correct decisions don't guarantee correct outcomes 100 percent of the time. Do you make the right move now? Even knowing it's right, it's still hard. That's why we need to revisit and continue exploring Unfortunate Truth #2.

WORKS CITED

BASF. 2019. *David Hula Breaks World Corn Yield Record.* https://agriculture.basf.us/crop-protection/news-events/stories-from-the-field/david-hula-breaks-world-corn-yield-record.html.

Ma, Jeff. 2010. *The House Advantage: Playing the Odds to Win Big in Business.* St. Martin's Press.

Ma, Jeff. 2019. *Jeff Ma—Keynote Presentation at BigSpeak Speakers Bureau.* Performed by Jeff Ma. February 20.

Widmar, Nicole J. Olynk, Michael L. Smith, and Erin Robinson. 2025a. *Consumer Corner: Decisions That Shape Supply Chains.* Purdue University Press.

Widmar, Nicole J. Olynk, Michael L. Smith, and Erin Robinson. 2025b. *Consumer Corner: Markets We Thought We Knew.* Purdue University Press.

Adapted from original posting as *ConsumerCorner.2022.Letter.24* (https://agribusiness.purdue.edu/consumer_corner/everything-is-just-math/)

18

THE TIME VALUE
OF MONEY

Y ou can hardly navigate online or step into a public space without being inundated with news about inflation, inflationary pressures, and what inflation is doing to you. There are many reasons for the situation, including geopolitical crises, ongoing wars, supply-side constraints, shifts in demand following the pandemic (or continuing in subsequent ways), energy market volatility, and labor market challenges. The list could go on. Interestingly, some even attempt to blame millennials, as if a single generation could somehow be at fault here. Millennials are to blame for sky-high inflation, one strategist says (Turak 2022). Bottom line is that there is no shortage of strife, speculation, and disagreement about the broader economy.

Amid all this chatter, and its real impacts on real households, remains the need for individuals to decide what to do with their money. Articles like "How to Invest When Inflation Is Bad and a Recession May Loom" and "Inflation Soared in June, Pinching Consumers and Challenging Policymakers" drive to the point that we still need to make decisions, spend money, procure goods, invest, save, and, well . . . live (Sommer 2022; Semialek 2022). Given that reality, it is worth revisiting the fundamentals: the time value of money.

Why is a dollar today worth more than a dollar tomorrow (or any time in the future)?

The most obvious reason is *inflation*. Simply stated, inflation means that the dollar will purchase fewer goods and services in the future.

Inflation is unfortunate, but compound interest (investing and earning interest, which compounds over time) is the side of this that we can take advantage of.

Inflation is not the only reason a dollar today is worth more than a dollar in the future. In fact, the time value of money rests on several principles, and some of them work to our advantage:

- Compound interest: By investing a dollar today, you can earn interest—and that interest compounds over time. This is the side of the equation we can use *for* us rather than against us.
- Opportunity cost: If you have the dollar today, you can invest it today and start earning interest on it. If you don't get the dollar until tomorrow, you've lost today's earning potential.
  - More broadly, every decision carries an opportunity cost. Whatever choice you make, you are sacrificing an alternative. I chose to spend my time writing this piece on the time value of money; therefore, I did not write about gerbils, goldfish, or anything else.
- Consumption value: A dollar today can buy goods or services you can enjoy now. Future dollars delay that consumption.
- Risk: Every future time period carries uncertainty. There's risk that I don't show up to give you the dollar tomorrow. There is risk that the mechanism designed to transfer rights to the dollar from me to you tomorrow changes, fails, or ceases to exist. There's risk that you aren't here to collect it. The further into the future we go, the greater the uncertainty.

There is no shortage of media attention on job reports, employment stats, and consumer confidence indicators. But as consumers, producers, employees, and business owners, we must make decisions in the face of uncertainty. That makes it worthwhile to return to this "back to basics" lesson on the time value of money.

WORKS CITED

Semialek, Jeanna. 2022. "Inflation Soared in June, Pinching Consumers and Challenging Policymakers." nytimes.com/2022. July 13. https://www.nytimes.com/2022/07/13/business/economy/inflation-june-interest-rates.html.

Sommer, Jeff. 2022. "How to Invest When Inflation Is Bad and a Recession May Loom." nytimes.com/2022. July 14. https://www.nytimes.com/2022/07/14/business/investing-inflation-recession.html.

Turak, Natasha. 2022. "The Size of the Millennial Generation Is to Blame for Sky-High Inflation, Strategist Says." cnbc.com/2022. July 15. https://www.cnbc.com/2022/07/15/millennials-are-to-blame-for-sky-high-inflation-strategist-says.html.

Adapted from original posting as *ConsumerCorner.2022.Letter.27* (https://agribusiness.purdue.edu/consumer_corner/the-time-value-of-money/)

19

PROBABILITY IS DIFFERENT FROM PROPENSITY

P robability. It's a noun, and according to Dictionary.com, it is "the extent to which something is probable; the likelihood of something happening or being the case" (dictionary.com 2025). It's also defined as "a probable or the most probable event," and under the mathematics subheading, we get "the extent to which an event is likely to occur, measured by the ratio of the favorable cases to the whole number of cases possible."

No wonder humans struggle to understand—and especially to interpret and internalize—probabilities. It is confusing even by definition, and that's before we introduce idioms like *in all probability*, which apparently (but not clearly) means that something is very likely. At face value, however, *in all probability* sounds like we're saying all—as in 100 percent. That is certainty, not likelihood. Yet we toss around phrases like this and then wonder why we have trouble using or internalizing probability.

Revealing my own biases, I tend to think of probability as something such as "the probability of outcome *a*, given *b*, is *c*." Consider the Venn diagrams in Figure 19.1, often used to illustrate how to assess the probability

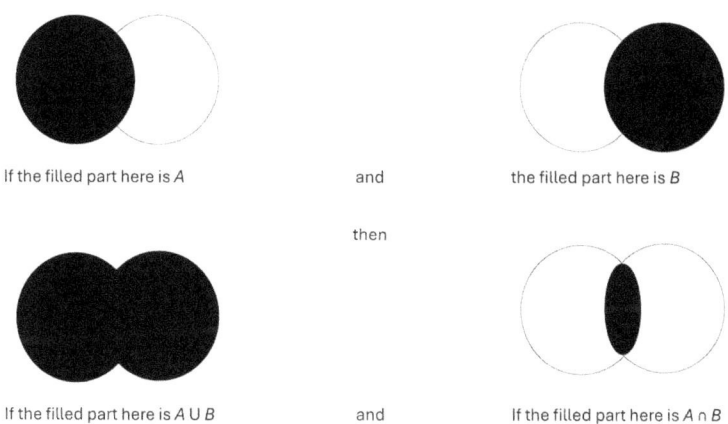

If the filled part here is *A*   and   the filled part here is *B*

then

If the filled part here is *A* ∪ *B*   and   If the filled part here is *A* ∩ *B*

FIGURE 19.1. Visual representations of the probability of events A and/or B occurring. Author's own illustration of common example from set theory.

of events occurring. We see the probability of one event (A) occurring without the other (B), and vice versa. We also see the probability of either A or B (or both) occurring (A ∪ B), as well as the probability of both events occurring together (A ∩ B), which is known as an intersection.

Most of us might prefer probability in the "Everything Is Just Math" sense, simply because it's straightforward (see chapter 17). But interpreting probabilities, not in the sense of how you do the math but more in the conceptual and philosophical sense, has been debated historically. This is not a new problem. It's one we've simply maintained.

Steven Pinker tackles probability versus propensity in his book *Rationality: What It Is, Why It Seems Scarce, Why It Matters* (Pinker 2022). In that book, Pinker explores the Monty Hall problem, which he also explains in detail in his article "Why You Should Always Switch: The Monty Hall Problem (Finally) Explained" (Pinker 2021). Pinker goes to great lengths to walk even the most skeptical reader through the probability of choosing the correct door and how those probabilities change as the game progresses, but admits that even some great mathematical minds hold out and don't agree. He then offers an explanation on why "people's insensitivity to this lucrative but esoteric information pinpoints the cognitive weakness at the heart of the puzzle: we confuse probability with propensity" (Pinker 2021).

Per Pinker, propensity is the disposition of an object to respond or behave in a given way—a human intuition based on physical characteristics. Borrowing Pinker's example, you may sense that a bent tree branch tends to spring back. "A propensity cannot be perceived directly (either the branch sprang back, or it didn't), but it can be inferred by scrutinizing the physical makeup of an object and working through the laws of cause and effect" (Pinker 2021). Of course, a drier branch may snap rather than spring back; we know that, too.

In contrast to propensity, probability can be updated with every tidbit of information. It's not just about knowledge of the branch or past experience; it's about reducing ignorance. Pinker argues that probabilities are not about the world itself but about our uncertainty regarding it. As uncertainty is resolved, probabilities change.

In 1959, Karl Popper wrote in "The Propensity Interpretation of Probability" in the *British Journal for the Philosophy of Science* that "mere possibilities could never give rise to any prediction" (Popper 1959). With that one phrase, our loose use of probability—as if it were interchangeable with a type of weather—falls apart. Pinker also tackles the forecasting problem and highlights a whole slew of challenges humans face when turning probabilities into predictions. He notes that the easier something is to visualize, the more likely it seems to us—a cognitive bias that should be concerning (especially on the heels of a conversation about probabilities and our challenges with using them correctly even in simple games). His point about forecasters often presenting vivid narratives, "probability be damned," underscores our vulnerability to stories over statistics. This takes us back to earlier concerns about data-driven decision-making in a world where everything is "just math."

Bottom line: Even when probabilities are known, we often fail to recognize or follow the optimal path—sometimes even when we think we can see it. Don't believe me? Revisit Pinker's Monty Hall discussion in "Why You Should Always Switch: The Monty Hall Problem (Finally) Explained" (Pinker 2021). The sooner we appreciate this gap, the sooner we can make real progress toward data-driven decisions, assuming that is something we truly want to do.

WORKS CITED

dictionary.com. 2025. "probability." dictionary.com/browse. https://www.dictionary.com/browse/probability.

Pinker, Steven. 2021. "Why You Should Always Switch: The Monty Hall Problem (Finally) Explained." *Behavioral Scientist.* October 4. https://behavioralscientist.org/steven-pinker-rationality-why-you-should-always-switch-the-monty-hall-problem-finally-explained/.

Pinker, Steven. 2022. *Rationality: What It Is, Why It Seems Scarce, Why It Matters.* Penguin Books.

Popper, Karl R. 1959. "The Propensity Interpretation of Probability." *British Journal for the Philosophy of Science* 10, no. 37, 25–42.

Adapted from original posting as *ConsumerCorner.2022.Letter.28* (https://www.agribusiness.purdue.edu/consumer_corner/probability-is-different-than-propensity-1/)

20

WHY DOES EVERYBODY KNOWING SOMETHING MAKE IT RIGHT?

T he challenge with consumers is that they aren't just walking around as these mythical, one-dimensional consumer-bots. They are thinking, feeling, and ever-changing human beings. Also lest you forget, *you* are one of these (problematic) creatures (Widmar 2021b).

If you've been following along, you may know we're fans of posing the deep philosophical questions here on *Consumer Corner* to better understand our humanness and how that extends to societal and consumer behaviors. Recall our deep dive into "Why Is a Raven Like a Writing Desk?" and the flashback to that same debate eighteen months later (spoiler alert: same result, but with fresh debate) (Widmar et al. 2025b, chapter 1; Widmar 2021a).

Well, we're back at it with a new inquiry—this one borrowed from Sheldon Cooper instead of Lewis Carroll: Why does everybody knowing something make it right?

The answer: It doesn't. Just because everybody "knows something" doesn't make it right. In fact, you should probably start asking: *Who is everybody, anyway?*

Even when it comes to football in Texas (which is a big deal!), everything is, in the end, just math. Picture this: It's football in Texas. Or, better yet, it's *Young Sheldon*, and we're watching Coach Cooper coach a high school football game (*Young Sheldon*, season 1, episode 5). The team is on the twelve-yard line. "Everybody knows you punt," right? But why does "everybody knowing something" make it right? Coach Cooper is going with his son, Sheldon, in making a decision for his football team. If you know Sheldon Cooper from *The Big Bang Theory* or *Young Sheldon*, you know Sheldon and football don't exactly mix. But here's the thing: it's not really about football—it's about the math and statistics.

Sheldon's mother, ever supportive, is in the bleachers sitting next to a particularly opinionated fan who shouts, "What the hell? Punt!" She responds, "Statistically, they're better off going for it." To which he fires back, "Says who?" The conversation continues from there, but you get the point.

Have you ever stopped to consider that when "everybody knows you punt," nobody ever asks who "everybody" is? In the show, the phrase gets repeated multiple times—by the coach, the assistant coach, Georgie Cooper (Sheldon's older brother)—yet not once does anyone stop to consider how everybody knows, who everybody is, or whether this so-called wisdom is even right in the first place (or at all).

If you think about it long enough, you might agree that young Sheldon is making the case for Unfortunate Truth #2, which we explored in "Don't Eat Random Mushrooms" (Widmar et al. 2025a, chapter 12): If we are going to make data-driven decisions, then we can no longer do whatever we want, what feels right, what our gut says to do, or what "everybody knows you should do." Instead, we may have to do things we might not necessarily *want to do.*

In short, everybody knowing something *does not* make it right. In fact, they (everybody) might not know it all (whatever it is).

WORKS CITED

Widmar, Nicole J. Olynk. 2021a. "Flashback: Let's Revisit the Raven and the Writing Desk." *Consumer Corner.* December 6. https://agribusiness.purdue.edu/consumer_corner/revisiting-the-raven-and-the-writing-desk/.

Widmar, Nicole Olynk. 2021b. "You Demanding, Fickle and (at Least Somewhat) Uninformed Consumer, You." *Consumer Corner.* June 7. https://agribusiness.purdue.edu/consumer_corner/you-demanding-consumer-you/.

Widmar, Nicole J. Olynk, Michael L. Smith, and Erin Robinson. 2025a. *Consumer Corner: Decisions That Shape Supply Chains.* Purdue University Press.

Widmar, Nicole J. Olynk, Michael L. Smith, and Erin Robinson. 2025b. *Consumer Corner: Markets We Thought We Knew.* Purdue University Press.

Young Sheldon. Season 1, episode 5, "A Solar Calculator, a Game Ball, and a Cheerleader's Bosom." Aired November 2, 2017, on CBS. Directed by Jay Chandrasekhar. Written by Chuck Lorre and Steven Molaro. https://www.paramountplus.com.

Adapted from original posting as *ConsumerCorner.2023.Letter.10* (https://agribusiness.purdue.edu/consumer_corner/why-does-everybody-knowing-something-make-it-right/)

21

MEEMAW'S MATH AND WHERE SHE WENT WRONG

In the last chapter, we tackled the *Young Sheldon*–inspired philosophical question, "Why does everybody knowing something make it right?" Spoiler: It doesn't. And you should probably be a little embarrassed that you've never even stopped to ask who "everybody" actually is. Everybody could be nobody, and even if it's somebody, who says they know anything?

Sheldon did not just advise his father, Coach Cooper, on football plays. He also gave advice to his Meemaw on sports gambling. Sitting in front of the TV with his family, he declared:

> Statistically, always punting on 4th down makes no sense. . . . When the Aggies give up the ball on their own five-yard line, the opposing team has a 92% chance of scoring. When they punt from deep in their own territory, the other team still has a 77% chance of scoring. But since they convert on 4th down 50% of the time, the math says they should never punt again. (*Young Sheldon*, season 1, episode 5)

Now, Meemaw had a few debts to settle and apparently a taste for betting, despite having placed a few wagers that didn't go so well. So she goes to tuck young Sheldon in for the night . . . and slips in a question: Could those statistics he was talking about with his dad be applied to next week's game? And could he tell her not only who would win but by how much?

Sheldon's answer: "I suppose with enough data that I could make a reasonable guess."

But Meemaw didn't want a guess—she wanted certainty. So she delivers Sheldon the data, only to find his analytics delayed because he has homework. After a rather un-grandma-like exchange in which Meemaw insinuates she's owed gambling tips because she makes him cookies, and Sheldon threatens to tell his mother about her gambling habit, Sheldon finally gives her pick: take the Oilers and gives the points.

Then, the Oilers lost.

Sheldon shares that Meemaw never asked for his help in these endeavors again. But here's the real question: Was Sheldon wrong? No, he wasn't. What we are facing here is a poor outcome from the right decision. It happens, because practically every decision we make is made under some degree of uncertainty.

As we discussed earlier, it's all just math, after all. For more perspective, let's draw inspiration from Jeff Ma's book *The House Advantage: Playing the Odds to Win Big in Business* (Ma 2010).

Imagine you're Jeff Ma, sitting at the blackjack table counting cards. You know what the math says you should do in this moment. But last time you made this exact same decision, you had a poor outcome. You know that doesn't matter, because even though the outcome was bad last time, the decision was mathematically correct. Given the uncertainty, the correct decision does not yield the correct outcome every time. You know the correct decision using a data-driven process is still the correct decision regardless of how you *feel* about it. Do you do the right thing?

We previously explored a related concept in "Don't Eat Random Mushrooms," specifically Unfortunate Truth #3 (Widmar et al. 2025, chapter 12): You cannot let the fear of a bad outcome stop you from making the right decision.

It is entirely possible to make the right decision and experience a bad outcome, and it's also possible to make the wrong decision and experience a good outcome. However, the outcome is not what we should be worried about in evaluating the decision. Instead, we need to separate the decision from the outcome. From Jeff Ma:

> I'm standing behind you, let's say next year in Vegas, you have a 16 and the dealer has a 9 up. And you say to me, hey Jeff, what did you say I was supposed to do here. I say, hey, you're supposed to hit. If you get a 5 to make 21 and win, I'm a genius, but if you get a 6 to get 22 and lose, I'm a moron that they never should have made a book or a movie about. But in both cases the decision was 100% correct; one was just a poor outcome and the other was a great outcome.

Meemaw tried to use math to win some money betting sports to pay back what were apparently previous gambles that did not go so well. Was she wrong? No, she was finally onto something. She was finally going to be data-driven. But one data-driven decision later, she suffered a poor outcome and quit using data. Her mistake, believe it or not, was not asking her grandson for gambling advice. Her mistake was abandoning a sound, data-driven strategy after one bad outcome.

WORKS CITED

Ma, Jeff. 2010. *The House Advantage: Playing the Odds to Win Big in Business.* St. Martin's Press.

Widmar, Nicole J. Olynk, Michael L. Smith, and Erin Robinson. 2025. *Consumer Corner: Decisions That Shape Supply Chains.* Purdue University Press.

Young Sheldon. "A Solar Calculator, a Game Ball, and a Cheerleader's Bosom." Season 1, episode 5. Aired November 23, 2017, on CBS. Directed by Jay Chandrasekhar. Written by Chuck Lorre and Steven Molaro. https://www.paramountplus.com.

Adapted from original posting as *ConsumerCorner.2023.Letter.12* (https://agribusiness.purdue.edu/consumer_corner/meemaws-math-and -where-she-went-wrong/)

22

ALL IS FAIR, SO LONG AS IT'S IN MY FAVOR

The topic of data ownership and acceptable use of data in agriculture has ignited fervent debate. For all the time, money, effort, and public discord, it isn't clear to me that we have even agreed on what data is (recall chapter 5). No wonder we cannot coalesce on how to use it.

When we consider photos, videos, buying or selling records, internet browsing history, and even social media under the expansive umbrella of data, it's always good to ask: Is it useful? I'm not sure. But data is being generated constantly—chances are you're reading this on your trusty iPhone, that faithful partner capable of locating your parked car, managing your passwords (even the ones you've forgotten), and suggesting your next purchase (okay, that's more Amazon via iPhone, but you get the idea).

Beyond the data's scale, scope, or quality lies the question of its accessibility.

"I know something you don't know" posited how information asymmetries are a contributing factor toward market failures (see chapter 12). With the growing availability of nontraditional data, like social media and online listening data, we've entered a new era of information accessibility. This inherently prompts us to wonder not only who has access but also their intentions for its use. Remember the GameStop situation?

When retail stock traders conspired online to pump up the price of the stock (WSJ 2021)? Later dubbed "the scandal that wasn't," it became a case study in how Web 2.0 capabilities, where everyone is both a content creator and a consumer, can exert a tangible influence on real-world markets. While we utterly and obviously missed the GameStop boat, our research has yielded wins, linking online media sentiments and volumes to stock performance (Widmar et al. 2025b, chapter 2). We've also linked online mentions of food-related illnesses and food safety to real-time CDC reports (Widmar et al. 2025b, chapter 11).

Agriculture has a deep-rooted tradition for valuing public information from the United States Department of Agriculture (USDA) and associated agencies. This publicly available data has played a pivotal role in building and sustaining the US agricultural and food markets into what they are today. But even with this leveling force of public information, a competitive race remains for privately available and restricted insights. We like data, and we want more, better, and faster access to it than everyone else.

Here's why Unfortunate Truth #2 (which we've revisited multiple times as it remains true) comes into play: "You can no longer do whatever you want to do, what feels right, or what your gut says to do. You may now have to do things you might not necessarily *want* to do, and that is really hard sometimes" (Widmar et al. 2025a, chapter 12).

Unless, of course, the data benefits us (especially if it benefits *me* more than *you*). In that case, we revisit our analyses, poke holes in the methodology, or declare an extenuating circumstance. Our cries for *data-driven decisions* quickly subside. In other words, we're all for fairness and talk a big game about following the data, until we have the chance to skew the game in our favor. Simply stated, "All is fair, so long as it's in my favor."

Online and social media data may feel "new," but the underlying concept isn't. Data concerning your purchasing habits, what you look at, what you search for, where you go, what you do, and so on is also data for decision-making. We all want more data. But more than that, we want more data for ourselves.

Exclusive crop tours, insider crop images, access to niche survey data all align with this theme—acquiring more information than others to gain a competitive advantage.

Once, this advantage came from physical observation; now, it's about leveraging streams of digital data. The central idea hasn't changed: Having more information than others creates advantage. The twist? The sheer volume of information available today often exceeds our capacity to process or even handle it—even if we had access to all of it. As a result, we object to inequalities quickly. What is fair and for whom? These questions will only grow more complicated as new possibilities emerge within these vast datasets.

WORKS CITED

Widmar, Nicole J. Olynk, Michael L. Smith, and Erin Robinson. 2025a. *Consumer Corner: Decisions That Shape Supply Chains.* Purdue University Press.

Widmar, Nicole J. Olynk, Michael L. Smith, and Erin Robinson. 2025b. *Market Signals from Online Behavior.* Purdue University Press.

WSJ. 2021. "The GameStop Scandal That Wasn't." *wsj opinion.* October 19. https://www.wsj.com/opinion/the-gamestop-scandal-that-wasnt-sec-gary-gensler-meme-stock-trading-11634680971.

Adapted from original posting as *ConsumerCorner.2023.Letter.21* (https://agribusiness.purdue.edu/consumer_corner/all-is-fair-so-long-as-its-in-my-favor/)

CONCLUSION
Rethinking Consumer Data and Behavior

R ecognizing the type of data you are working with is essential—and not just whether it is cross-sectional, time series, or panel data. Consider whether it was collected from equipment taking measurements, or self-reported by people. Bias is everywhere and while it can be recognized and maybe even accounted for to some degree, it cannot be eliminated. We always remember the extremes and seldom recall the "normal" days. We inherently want to protect ourselves and our own egos and have a hard time reporting on our own "bad." Asking people to self-report their New Year's resolutions on January 1 is one thing. Asking people on January 31 how many days they actually went to the gym in January is another. Are they supposed to just remember? If so, do you think days for which we are uncertain are more likely to get a probably yes or a probably no? Do you think it matters who is asking the question and how we need to report it? Even the mode of collection—online, on paper, or face-to-face—matters. And if it's face-to-face, the identity of the person asking matters too. The short answer? Yes, all of it influences the data.

Collecting data is important, but understanding the contexts in which data was collected is also important. Machines might be less sensitive to such biases, but humans design, control, and interpret them. They can be unplugged at any time.

Everything around us is math—or at least quantifiable in some probabilistic sense. Fans of *Young Sheldon* will recall that you can use statistics to make football decisions, or as Meemaw discovered, betting decisions. Her mistake wasn't turning to data. It was quitting after one bad outcome from a sound decision. Like Meemaw, we're enthusiastic about data-driven decisions, until the data asks us to do something uncomfortable. Then, suddenly, the model is flawed (or so we say).

One of the most unfortunate truths about data-driven decision-making is that you may be asked to do things you *don't want* to do. And that is hard.

Data quality adds another layer of complexity. Garbage in, garbage out. No model can fix flawed inputs. Yet, we rarely argue about how reliable a dataset is, except when the results don't favor us. If the outcome benefits us, we stop asking questions. After all, all is fair—so long as we win.

Too often, we underinvest in consistent, unbiased data collection, compromising the integrity of future analyses—some of which haven't even been imagined yet. If we care about insights that matter, the integrity of our data must come first.

Consumer Corner won't stop exploring novel data sources, evolving uses, market insights, and resilience-building strategies. Because consumers (you!)—fickle, demanding, and often seemingly uninformed—will always keep us guessing.

ABOUT THE AUTHORS

Nicole J. Olynk Widmar is an agricultural economist specializing in farm businesses and consumer decision-making under uncertainty. She serves as a professor and the head of the Department of Agricultural Economics at Purdue University.

Michael L. Smith is a research scientist specializing in the human dimensions of resource use, applying cross-disciplinary methods in agricultural economics and the social sciences. He works in Purdue University's Department of Agricultural Economics.

Erin Robinson is a communications and marketing professional with experience in agricultural business and academic research environments. As marketing manager for Purdue University's Center for Food and Agricultural Business, she develops marketing strategies, creates content and outreach initiatives, drives brand awareness, and evaluates marketing effectiveness.

ABOUT THE CONTRIBUTORS

F. Bailey Norwood holds the Barry Pollard, MD P&K Equipment Professorship of Agribusiness at Oklahoma State University. As a researcher Bailey has published studies on a variety of topics including food insecurity during COVID, the impact of wheat varieties on the taste of bread, and the philosophy of why we garden.

Courtney Bir, associate professor of Agricultural Economics at Oklahoma State University, holds a PhD from Purdue and master's and bachelor's degrees from OSU. Her research examines consumer preferences for agricultural products and production economics, aiming to align preferences with profitability. Her extension work focuses on farm finance and operational goal achievement.

Brenna Ellison is a professor of Agribusiness Management and the Undergraduate Programs coordinator in the Department of Agricultural Economics at Purdue University. Her research focuses on how consumers make food choices, including what consumers choose not to eat, or waste. Ellison earned her BS in Agribusiness from Abilene Christian University and her MS and PhD in Agricultural Economics from Oklahoma State University.

Melissa L. Reed is a postdoctoral fellow in the Department of Entomology and Plant Pathology at Oklahoma State University. Her research spans aquatic insect ecology, student perceptions of entomology, and the role of gender in science education. Reed has published studies on topics such as macroinvertebrate diversity in Oklahoma streams, the use of recycled materials for insect sampling, and college students' willingness to consume insects.

Audrey Ruple is the Dorothy A. and Richard G. Metcalf Professor of Veterinary Medical Informatics at the Virginia-Maryland College of Veterinary Medicine at Virginia Tech. Ruple joined Virginia Tech in 2021 as an associate professor of quantitative epidemiology with tenure, focusing on informatics and its application to veterinary medicine. Ruple is a Diplomate of the American College of Veterinary Preventive Medicine and a Member of the Royal College of Veterinary Surgeons.

Camille (Cami) Ryan, BComm, PhD, is a Bayer Science fellow, a professional affiliate with the College of Agriculture at the University of Saskatchewan, and senior business partner for Industry Affairs and Sustainability with Bayer CropScience Canada. With a broad academic and professional background in social sciences and economics, Ryan passionately advocates for policy based on science-based evidence in the agriculture industry.

Jeffrey Young is an assistant professor of Agribusiness Economics at Murray State University. His favorite classes to teach are econometrics, industrial organization, and ag finance. His research focuses on the economics of education, simulation methods, spatial problems in production ag markets, and empirical game theory. He also helps out on his 4,700-acre family row crop farm in western Kentucky, professionally consults in economic impact analysis and forensic economics, and writes for ag-focused audiences for *Agricultural Economic Insights* and other outlets.